Never a Mother to Me

Also by bestselling author Tracy Black:

Never a Hero to Me

Never a Mother to Me

TRACY BLACK

with Linda Watson-Brown

SIMON &
SCHUSTER

London · New York · Sydney · Toronto · New Delhi

A CBS COMPANY

First published in Great Britain by Simon & Schuster UK Ltd, 2013
A CBS company

Copyright © 2013 Tracy Black and Linda Watson-Brown

1 3 5 7 9 10 8 6 4 2

Simon & Schuster UK Ltd
1st Floor
222 Gray's Inn Road
London WC1X 8HB

www.simonandschuster.co.uk

Simon & Schuster Australia,
Sydney

Simon & Schuster India,
New Delhi

A CIP catalogue record for this book is available from the British Library

Paperback Original ISBN: 978-1-47110-273-8
eBook ISBN: 978-1-47110-274-5

Typeset by Hewer Text UK Ltd, Edinburgh
Printed and bound in the UK by CPI (UK) Ltd, Croydon CR0 4YY

To my partner, who has helped me to keep looking forwards and not backwards.

For my ever-increasing family: my children, my new daughter-in-law and grandchildren, who I love so dearly.

ABOUT THE AUTHOR

Tracy Black published her first book in 2011. Although she had been terrified that no one would believe her, she took the brave step of going public with her horrific story of abuse and betrayal in *Never a Hero to Me*.

She was then inundated with supportive emails and also requests to continue with her story, offering hope to many other survivors who saw parallels with their own experiences, and who wanted to know how Tracy had managed to turn her life around.

Tracy has continued with her travels since the publication of her first book and after some time in the Far East, is now back in Europe, where she lives with her long-term partner. She has become a grandmother recently and continues to support survivors of abuse.

Tracy Black is a pseudonym. Names have been changed to protect anonymity.

CONTENTS

FOREWORD

It has been two years since I spoke out. Of course, before that, I had told people about all the awful things my father had done to me; I had told them as a child, and I had told them as an adult. But I had always been constrained: by time, by the expectations of others, by my own need to keep some things to myself. When I wrote my first book, I felt as if I was finally expressing myself in a way that made sense. It was on my terms and in my words.

I had no idea then what would happen. It was, in many ways, a terrifying thing to do, despite the fact that I had wanted to do it for so long. I wanted to break the silence that defines the world of the abused child and the adult they become, but I knew there would be a reaction – not being able to gauge in advance what that reaction would involve was scary, but I knew the truth had to be told. I'm so glad that I took the chance.

I think anyone reading this who has been abused will understand the fear I felt. Did I want to bring all of this out into the open and, if I did, would anyone believe me? There had really only ever been one person who had believed me – the Commanding Officer of the Army base I grew up on – and I fully trust that, in believing me, he saved me. By getting me out of my horrific home life and sending me to a boarding school, organised and funded by the Army, he gave me an escape route from my father and the terrible things he was doing to me. The sad fact was that there was no escape from myself.

When I knew that the book was finally going to happen, that I was finally going to get to tell the truth, there was a little voice inside me that said:

No one will believe you.

They'll say you're a liar.

They'll say you're making it all up.

They'll say it's some sick fantasy.

They'll say your dad was a hero.

To the outside world, my dad was a respectable Army soldier, a good and honourable man. But he was never a hero to me. The sick fantasy was his, not mine. Even years after his death, he still had a hold on me, because that little voice inside made me question myself, just as he had done for so long. What many people don't realise is that the fight doesn't stop when you leave home, or when your abuser dies, or even if there is a conviction and some form of justice. The fight doesn't end with any of those things, because it goes on inside you. When a child is abused, their childhood is stolen forever; and an adult who has had their childhood stolen can become a lost soul.

I know I was.

I had never been loved by either of my parents. My father sexually abused me within a hideous framework of manipulation and emotional blackmail; my mother showed me no love and no compassion.

If that is your childhood, what kind of adult will you grow up to be?

I think it's in our own hands to decide the people we become, and I decided to become a good one. We all make our own choices. My parents did, and when I was a mother, I chose to be a loving, supportive one, a mother who was always there for her boys. It wasn't easy, and it is the story of my years after the abuse ended that seems to have made readers want to contact me. So many of them wanted to know more of the details I only touched on in the final chapters of *Never a Hero to Me*, and all the people who contacted me had questions.

Do you have any relationship with your mother?

What happened when you had children?

Have you put your past behind you?

Do you still think of what he did to you?

What's the rest of the story, Tracy, what's the rest of the story?

As time went on, I realised that there was still so much to tell. Many people wanted to know what had happened after the last chapter, many of them said they desperately wanted to know if I'd had the happy ending they hoped for me. I couldn't answer any of the questions in a quick email, not really. There was no efficient summary of the rest of my life, no swift one-liner to pull the rest of my tale together. Slowly, it dawned on me – *I needed to write another book.*

The difference for me when writing this second book has been you – the reader. The story of the rest of my life would never have seen the light of day were it not for the outpouring of love and support I received from the people who had read my story. I received so many messages from the very first day my book was published, and every single person who got in contact believed me. Readers who had never been abused said that it had opened their eyes. Other survivors thanked me for speaking out and making them realise that they were not alone. I was so touched that people had taken the time to write, to write to *me*. The fact that they had chosen to read my story and had believed me meant so much. When I first began this journey, I had thought that getting my book published would mark the end of it all, but in fact it was only the beginning. It became so clear to me that I hadn't just helped myself by telling the world what had happened to me, I had actually helped other people too. They had been silenced just like me, and they were now taking strength from the parts of my story they could relate to. By speaking out, I was in some way giving them a voice too.

As you read each chapter, I hope that you take strength from what I tell you. I got through the tough times and if, like me, you are also a survivor of abuse, you got through them too. Just because survivors have scars, just because we sometimes find it hard to keep going, it doesn't mean we're weak. We've already been through more than most people can ever imagine, but we have stayed strong and we still fight every single day. It's a constant battle, and there are so many casualties, but I'm proud to still be standing and hope that you feel the same way. I have taken so much strength from the love that I have been inundated with in the past two years; by opening my heart and unlocking my memory again, I hope that I can give back some of the incredible support I've received.

So, here it is. This is my story: of the deepest, darkest abuse which I couldn't bear to cover in my first book, of the effect it had on me as I took my first tentative steps towards adulthood, of how I negotiated the minefield of being a wife, mother and woman while carrying the burden of a sick and twisted childhood.

After this, there's no more to tell.

CHAPTER 1

WHAT'S WRONG?

When I was a little girl – like all little girls, and little boys – I wished for a lot of things but, on this particular day, I wished that I was just a bit taller. It was my fourth birthday and I thought I would have grown. I thought I would have sprouted into a big girl overnight. It hadn't happened and I knew for a fact that it hadn't happened because the button in the lift that I was trying to press was as far away today as it had been yesterday, or the day before.

I jumped up as high as I could and finally managed to press it after a few tries. It felt as if the door was taking forever to open, and I kept looking behind me, looking to see if anyone knew I had gone. Looking to see, more than anything, if Mum had even noticed I had disappeared. The lobby was empty. We lived in a block of flats in Singapore where lots of Army families were crammed together, and every floor looked the same. You could see right along the lobby to the entrance of every flat and it was deserted.

1

There was only me. Four years old today and running away.

'You can do this, Tracy,' I told myself, but my heart was pounding and I knew that I would be in so, so much trouble if I got caught. Inside the lift, I pressed the first button that came to hand and my stomach got a funny lurching as the journey began. We – the lift and I – were going down. That was fine, I wanted to get outside, get away from everything that was so wrong, but when the doors opened I realised it had taken me too far. Instead of being at ground level, I was in the basement.

I stepped out into the huge echoing space and looked around. I ran as fast as I could over to a wall where cars were all parked in a line facing out. Crouching behind them, it wasn't long before the tears started to fall. Everything was getting worse. It didn't feel like my birthday, it just felt like another horrible day.

There had been no presents for me that morning. I had only known that it was my birthday at all because my big brother Gary had been taunting me for days.

'You might be getting older, but you're getting stupider too!' he'd laugh.

'Do you know what you're getting for your birthday?' Gary would question me. 'Nothing! Nothing, nothing, nothing!'

It looked as if he was right. There were no balloons up on the walls of our flat, no pile of gifts, not even a card from Mum and Dad. Gary went off to school and Dad was at work, so I was there with Mum when she shoved a bowl of breakfast cereal towards me.

What's Wrong?

'Eat that and, for God's sake, don't make a mess,' she snarled.

She couldn't have said anything *more* likely to cause me to become nervous and start spilling the milk and sugary shapes as I tried to eat. By the time she turned round again from the sink, the table had quite a few puddles of milk, which I was desperately trying to scoop up with my spoon.

'Christ! Again! Is there ANYTHING you can do without making a mess? Is there?' she shouted.

Mum's face was really close to mine, and I started to shake. She was so angry these days. I could never predict what would set her off, but I did know that it was all my fault. It was because I was stupid. And slow. And needy. And demanding. And difficult. And thick. And clumsy. And lots and lots of other words that she hurled at me all day long.

'Wait till your father gets home!'

Those were the words she generally finished on, and the threat of that phrase always put the fear of God into me. I can't put my finger on why, but I do know that I was never sure what to expect. At that stage, Dad didn't shout at me – he left all the discipline issues to Mum (at that point, she was the only one who swore and she did plenty of it), so I would wonder what the result would be if he did ever take over when I was naughty. I was scared, very scared, and knew that I had to get out of the house, far away from there by the time he was due home. I had a feeling in me that I couldn't quite work out, and it felt physical as well as emotional. I think I had a sense that 'something' would happen because 'something' had happened before, but at such a young age I didn't have the words to identify what that 'something' was.

This is one of the half-heard whispers in my head. If Mum was the one who imposed the discipline, and if Dad wasn't violent and never swore at me during those times, why was I so scared of what he might do? It is so frustrating to not have the answers and to know that I'll never have them. I don't have the whole story of my own life. All I can do is work with what I *do* have, and those parts tell me that I was so scared of something I couldn't define in relation to my dad that I ran away when I was tiny and in a foreign country, because it was better than facing *that*, whatever *that* was.

I had sneaked out when Mum was busy with someone in the kitchen and I was so proud of myself for getting away, but once the doors opened onto that basement, my pride disappeared. I had been there before, with Mum, as it was where the caretaker had his workshop, and where he lived with his wife. They were always lovely to me but, as I hid behind the cars, I saw no sign of them and I couldn't stop the fear which ran through me.

'I'll be good, I'll be good,' I whispered to myself, 'just make Mum come for me. Make someone nice come for me.' I was regretting running away, but I was also too petrified to simply walk back to the lift and go home. The sad truth was, Mum had probably not even noticed my absence and, had I been able to get in the front door, she would have been none the wiser. However, the prospect of coming out of my hiding place and making that journey seemed impossible, so I stayed hidden, terrified, shaking, making vague promises to myself about being 'good', and praying that I would be found.

I could hear nothing, no sign of the caretaking couple, so I hid for what seemed like hours. It probably wasn't that long at all, but it seemed like a lifetime. As I waited, the air was extremely humid and dusty. I was terrified, so I just sat on my haunches and cried; I didn't feel there was anything else I *could* do. All I knew was that I didn't want to see my dad under any circumstances. I could cope with Mum, I could cope with her shouting and telling me I was stupid, but I most definitely did not want to be at his mercy when he came home.

I was finally found by the caretaker and his wife, who came across me sitting on the floor by his desk. In his broken English the caretaker told me that Mum was very worried.

'Come,' the man said to me. 'It's your birthday! Come!'

He led me by the hand as his wife smiled and said 'cake!' over and over again. Before we returned to my apartment, the couple took me to their flat where there was indeed a beautiful cake waiting for me.

'Cake!' the woman said again, and they both told me over and over again that it was my birthday. Smiling and happy, they were the exact opposite of what I was used to.

Once we had collected the cake, the woman took me by the hand this time and we all went back up in the lift. They were both lovely people, local to the area, and so kind to all the Army kids who lived there, often giving us fruit or sweets; I remember once being given chocolate shaped like little ants! I was glad they had found me, but I would have been even happier if I had been able to stay with them.

The man knocked on the door and Mum opened it.

'You silly girl, where have you been?' she said breezily. She seemed totally indifferent – neither angry or sad – just unbothered really, and yet I must have been away for ages because Dad was in the sitting room, back from work.

He threw a brief 'thanks' to the caretaker couple and went back to watching TV. I'd stopped crying by now, but I was still very upset to be back home. The kindly couple were still being lovely and they insisted on having a photo-graph taken with me and the cake they had made. I don't have this photo any more, but I do remember standing between them, holding the beautiful cake (which was the loveliest thing I'd been given that day), but being upset and tear-stained. I just didn't want to be back at home, and I was very unhappy.

The rest of the day was uneventful I think, but Dad glowered throughout the whole time and never said a word. There was always a sense of danger in the air, even if he never spoke to me directly or did anything in particular.

Back in Singapore, I was always on edge around Mum and Dad, but for different reasons. She was often angry, often shouting, never happy with me; Dad's was a quieter presence, his silence somehow seemed to be a greater threat. What I did know was that Mum loved my big brother. Gary was nearly three years older than me and she thought the sun rose and set with him. I don't recall her shouting at Gary, her only words for him were kindly, loving ones. She would ruffle his hair, cuddle him, kiss him, tell him he was handsome, tell him he was clever and smart. Through Gary I could see that Mum was capable of love, capable of being a good mother – just not with me. Given what she told me about my own failings, there was a clear reason for this: I was a bad little girl. Mum spent most of her time telling me that I was a drain on her, that I wore her out and that she wished she'd never had me. If he was there, Gary would smirk in the background, then turn into her little angel when she looked his way.

The building we lived in during our time in Singapore was really high; when I was four I thought the floor we lived on – the twenty-second – touched the sky. There was no play area for kids and Dad wouldn't allow me or my brother outside to play anywhere else. Mum had exactly the opposite attitude – when Dad wasn't around, she couldn't wait for us to go outside. She had very few friends back then, and was ill quite often, passing her time with jigsaws and knitting – things that kept her busy without wearing her out.

'Go outside and entertain yourself – I need a rest from all your racket,' she'd often tell me, sitting down wearily. She would never say that to Gary though, when he was at home during the holidays – she was never dismissive of him as she was of me. When Mum was looking after us, we would be allowed to play downstairs if we stayed within sight of the balcony, so she could wave us in whenever it was time for Dad to come back, usually five minutes after we got in. Sometimes we would stray from the building, but my brother had a built-in sensor, a 'Mum alert' he called it, and we would always be in her sight when she looked out. Due to Gary's 'Mum alert' we never got caught when we strayed.

Gary and I used to have to find our own way to play, and he particularly liked to chase rats along the sewer that ran outside the building. We used to place our feet on either side of the sewer and run along it with sticks in an attempt to whack the rats (I don't think we ever managed to hit one). One day, I slipped and fell into the middle of it and ended up filthy, all slimy and muddy, not to mention absolutely stinking! I went straight home, crying and feeling sore after my fall. Both my knees were bleeding, as was one of my elbows. I had to get the caretaker to hit the lift button as I was too small to reach it; I could only reach the bottom one that led to the basement. My brother stayed out to play as he wasn't that bothered about me and had said I was a 'cry baby' anyway.

Mum was really house-proud and didn't like anything to be messed up or dirty in the flat. When she saw me standing there, dripping all over the place, she was furious. I desperately wanted some sympathy and for her to kiss away the hurt, but there was no chance of that. She started screaming as soon as she saw the state of me at the door.

'What the fuck have you done now?' she yelled.

What's Wrong?

'I fell, Mum, and I've hurt myself,' I wept, going towards her.

'Get away from me!' she shouted. 'Get your arse into the bathroom and clean up – fucking move it!'

She grabbed my arm in disgust, practically pulling it from the socket, and dragged me into the bathroom, holding me as far away from her as possible.

'Get undressed,' she hissed as she started running the shower water, 'and don't you dare touch anything, not with those filthy hands.' I did as she said, still shaken from my fall and the sight of blood on my knees. I got into the shower and under the water, but as soon as I did, I scrambled to get out again – the water was scalding hot. As I tried desperately to get out from under the stream, Mum pushed me roughly back in and yelled, 'Stay there, you bastard!'

'But it's boiling, Mum, it's too hot!' I cried.

'Well, that will teach you to get into such a state then,' she screeched. I realised then that she meant for the temperature to be that hot. She meant to teach me a lesson. Mum kept me there for a couple of minutes longer, blocking my exit and telling me how stupid I was for ruining my clothes. 'And don't think you'll be getting a new skirt, just because you've got that one filthy and torn. Now go and put your pyjamas on and sit in your room until dinnertime. I don't want to hear a sound out of you until then.'

My body felt raw due to the heat of the water and it stung my knees. Not once did she attend to my cuts and grazes, no plasters were given to me and definitely no sympathy. She didn't even take the time to ask me how or where it had happened.

She did take pleasure in telling Dad when he came home, though. As he walked in the door and hung up his coat, she came out of the kitchen to relay to him the latest mischief I'd got myself into.

'Look at what this useless girl has done,' she told him. 'She's been busy making a nuisance of herself again, cutting her knees and wanting comforting for her own clumsiness.' Dad looked at me as I stood in the doorway of my bedroom, but said nothing – he didn't shout at me, or reprimand me physically, just shrugged his shoulders and went to the kitchen to get a beer from the fridge.

I wasn't allowed outside to play for another couple of weeks, but what most upset me about it all was the way Mum had been so cruel and unconcerned by my injuries and my tears. Why had she been so mean to me, why had she been so uncaring? I couldn't understand why she didn't try and make my scrapes better, like I had seen other mummies do, and the way I desperately wanted her to.

Mum had other problems too. Not only did she have me to put up with, but she was also suffering from a rare medical condition that would go undiagnosed for many years – for decades in fact. At that time, no one knew what was wrong with her, and though she was a lovely-looking woman, she was plagued by violent bouts of vomiting and pain, during which time her body would be covered in weeping sores.

What's Wrong?

Mum's illness blighted her life hugely, and it had far-reaching repercussions for me too. It's by her periods of illness that I can work out other things from my early years, and I know two things for certain. The first is that Mum had been ill for as long as I could remember. By the time I turned five, we had left Singapore and moved to West Germany, and although I had been sad to leave the friendly caretaker and his wife, I hoped that the doctors in Germany would be able to make Mum's sickness go away. But the doctors there were as baffled as the doctors in Singapore had been. I would hear her call out from her room to my dad: 'Harry! Harry! It's starting again, help me, Harry, dear God, help me!' There was no doubt that she was in tremendous pain and it was very hard to watch her suffer so much. Though the doctors on the Army base we had moved to in Rinteln ran lots of tests and tried to come up with a solution, Mum had to be taken into hospital when things were really bad, then come back home after a few days or weeks, seemingly better, only for the whole process to begin all over again. I was little, but I was observant. When I started to smell the creams that she would rub all over her skin, I knew she'd be unwell again soon. When she had even less time for me than usual, I knew it was because she needed to see the doctors. When I heard the retching noises and saw her face turn grey, I knew that it would soon be just me, Dad and Gary at home, while Mum went away to 'get better'.

I used to pray for her at night when I went to bed. *Please make my mummy better*, I'd whisper. *Please make the sickness*

11

stop, then she will feel better and then she will love me more because she won't feel so ill all the time. But Mum continued to be ill, and she continued to berate me. 'Is it any wonder I'm fucking sick all the time when I've got you to look after?' she'd yell, even on good days. 'As if it's not bad enough to carry the burden of this . . . I've got you constantly at me as well.' This was one of Mum's repeated complaints – that I was a burden, that I was always 'at' her, but the truth was, I was just a little girl who wanted her mummy. I adored her, even though she had no time for me, and I waited for the day when she would love me as much as she loved Gary. Her illness didn't seem to be made worse by him, yet she said that I made everything so much harder for her.

The second thing I know for certain is that one stormy night, when I was just five years old, Mum was hospitalised after a particularly bad attack of sickness, and from that point on Dad changed forever. I was an optimistic child, and I started each day thinking of the good things that might happen and focusing on what I liked most. That night, after dinner, I sat at the table and tried to do my homework. I hadn't been at school for long, but I was desperate to be a big girl, to be clever and read whatever book took my fancy. I concentrated as hard as I could as I tried to practise my writing, but I could hear Gary laughing at me.

'What is it, Gary?' I asked. 'Why are you laughing at me?'

He snatched up my homework book and said, 'You're stupid! I'm laughing at you because you're stupid!'

What's Wrong?

I could feel tears springing to my eyes, partly because I wondered if he was right – Gary was my big brother and if he said I was stupid, maybe I was? Dad did nothing to help, he just kept staring at the TV and smoking as he drank from beer cans which he threw into a box at the side of 'his' chair when empty. I grabbed my book from Gary and went to find Mum.

'Mum! Mum!' I wept, but as I pushed open her bedroom door, I saw that she was a long way from being able to interfere in a sibling squabble. Mum was bent in half over a basin, vomiting violently, convulsing in pain. I backed out of the room – this was awful. She'd been ill before, but this seemed worse than usual. Back in the lounge, Gary was still smirking, Dad sitting where I'd left him – they seemed completely oblivious to the horror Mum was going through. I stood there, watching them both and then, suddenly, Dad swivelled round and glared at me.

'Have you been harassing your mother?' he snarled.

'I just went to see . . .' I began.

'Well, for fuck's sake, leave her alone,' he interrupted.

This shocked me. Mum often swore, but not Dad. He wasn't a warm person and he believed that Army standards should always take precedence, but he never used that sort of language in front of me as a rule.

'What are you fucking gawping at? You know she isn't well, you know she's ill, and Christ knows when she'll get any better,' he snapped.

I'm not sure I did know that. At five, I just thought that one day she would be fine and she'd turn into a nice mummy.

'Keep the fuck away from her,' he continued, 'and get to bed.'

I grabbed my things and ran to my room, crying my heart out. Just as I threw myself on the bed, I heard a horrendous crack and saw flashes of light. The thunderstorm made me feel even worse, as if I was in the middle of a nightmare. I had been scared of storms for as long as I could remember, but now I had to pluck every ounce of courage in my body to go back through to Dad and beg to be allowed to stay at his side until this passed.

'I'm scared,' I whispered as I stood by his chair, hoping that his previous bad temper would have passed and he would see that he just needed to comfort a scared little girl. 'When will it stop, Dad?'

He wouldn't even make eye contact with me.

'Shut up. Get back to bed. Stop being so fucking annoying.'

'But, Dad—'

'Shut the fuck up. I mean it. Get back to bed and don't even think of bothering me again.'

But I had to try, I had to bother him again.

'Please, Dad, please,' I begged.

Finally, he turned round and looked at me. His stare was cold; there was a dead look in his eyes and it was almost as if he didn't even recognise his own child standing in front of him. The swearing, the aggression, the lack of any emotion – perhaps they were part of his life in the Army, but his behaviour was something I had never experienced before. It was as if something had broken in my father that night. This time, when he told me to go, I went.

As I lay in my bed that night watching the lightning dance on the nearby buildings, I shook with fear – a fear that came from a combination of natural childish terror at the awful weather and the sickness of my mum, as well as complete bafflement as to why Dad was suddenly swearing at me and making me feel so bad. Had something happened to him too? He had never been an attentive or fun dad, preferring to sit in his chair with a can of beer and a pile of empties in a cardboard box at the side of him. He would chain-smoke Senior Service cigarettes and stare at the television, but he didn't swear at us and he wasn't violent; in fact, until that night, I thought I was invisible to him.

When I woke up later that night, I thought at first that the bright colours I could see were from lightning flashes – when I realised they came from an ambulance, I stumbled to the door just as the ambulance men were taking Mum away. I could see Dad and Gary, and I could also hear a neighbour of ours called Agnes Anderson. I liked Agnes very much, so I wormed my way in between her and Dad.

'Let me take the kids for the night, Harry,' I heard her say. 'You've got enough on your plate.'

Dad was staring at me, his gaze unflinching as he replied, 'No, they're staying here.' He was so calm, so seemingly unaffected by the fact that his wife was being rushed away to hospital in the middle of the night, and so very sure that we would not be leaving with Agnes. I felt a panic rising in me, and I think Agnes sensed it too for she tried again, saying, 'Well, at least let me take Tracy; she looks terrified, poor wee thing.'

'Please let me go with Agnes!' I begged. Dad stared at me for a couple of seconds, holding my hand too tightly as they shut the ambulance doors. 'I've told you, no,' he said at last, his voice flat. 'You're staying with me.' My heart sank – it was almost as if somewhere inside I knew that Agnes was my only hope, and that if she left me there that evening, life would change forever.

I ran through to my bed that night, and lay with my arms wrapped around myself as tightly as possible, praying desperately that everything would be better in the morning.

I woke the next morning to the sound of Dad swearing yet again.

'Up! Up! Fucking move it!' he shouted. 'Get your arse through to breakfast now!'

It's hard to describe the sense of absolute confusion I felt as my life suddenly went into freefall. I was even more confused when I got to the kitchen. There was no breakfast laid out on the table. No sooner had I asked, 'Where is it then, Dad?' than I felt his hand slap the back of my head so hard that my forehead banged against the wooden table.

'Your breakfast will be there when you fucking make it,' he said. Dad had never hit me before – but he had never used bad language in front of me before last night either, and now he was doing that all of the time. Stunned and shocked, I was even more bewildered when he told me to make something for Gary too, as well as a cup of tea for him. I was five years old – I'd never used a kettle before, never made a meal, never done anything more than hold imaginary tea parties. 'You're the woman of the house now, Tracy,' he told me. 'Now make me a cup of fucking tea.'

I was scared, but I didn't want to risk being hit again so I knew I would have to try and be good, try to do everything he asked of me. Somehow, through balancing on stools and being very careful, I did manage to get cornflakes and milk into bowls, and even brewed a cup of tea. There was no triumph in it, I didn't feel proud or a big girl, I just felt the red mark burning on my forehead. I got through breakfast without being belted by Dad again, but I was shaking and terrified. I just wanted Mum back. Even if she shouted at me, I was familiar with that shouting, I knew what she was like; I didn't recognise Dad at all.

After Dad told me to clear the table, and I had managed to climb onto the stool again to put the dishes in the sink, I ran to my room to get ready for school – it had taken me a lot longer to do all the things Mum could do unthinkingly, and I was worried I would be late. Hurriedly, I got dressed and tried to brush my tangled hair, and then I ran out of the door.

When I got back from school later that afternoon, I fully expected Mum to be there, but my heart sank when I realised Dad was there alone. He told me that Mum was being kept in hospital, but he didn't seem upset. Gary was out playing football with his friends and, again, Dad seemed unbothered. In fact, when I told him that I'd seen my brother busy with his mates, he responded with a smile.

'Good,' he said, 'that gives us time.'

'Time for what, Dad?' I asked.

He paused, then replied, 'Follow me.'

I did – I was quickly getting used to doing everything he said – and Dad walked towards the bedroom he shared with Mum. Smiling, he told me, 'We'll change the bed, get all the sick off it from when Mum was ill. Go on. Strip the bed.' His demeanour seemed to have changed yet again, because he was smiling broadly now. I had never changed bedding before, I was far too little. I worried that it could be another trap – if I got this wrong, would his fists fly? He'd offered no help with breakfast so I assumed he would offer no help now either, but I was wrong. As if he could read my thoughts, he said he would show me exactly what to do. Even better, he said that he would tell Mum I'd done it all on my own and she would be very proud of me. I started smiling too – I'd like that, I really would.

He started to give me directions, telling me to open up the buttons, pull the quilt out, put the soiled cover in the washing basket. It was really hard work but I loved that he seemed happy, so I kept working, taking off the sheet and pillowcases as well.

'Well done, Tracy,' he said. 'Now here comes the fun part!'

He told me that putting on the clean cover was much harder than removing the dirty one, but he also said that he would help me. 'Stand in front of me,' he said, still smiling, as he shook the clean cover out. He put his arms around me and told me to grasp the two corners he was holding.

'I'll put the quilt in and you grab it once the cover is in place. This is fun, isn't it?' he asked, still smiling. But something had changed – when I craned my neck to look up at his face, his smile didn't seem quite right, and it didn't seem like fun at all because he was pressing into the back of me so hard.

It felt wrong.

It felt wrong from the start.

I told him I had the duvet cover, I told him that I didn't need his help any more, but it made no difference. He kept pushing into me, harder and harder. I was so little and my head was at the level of his crotch as he shoved into me.

'Dad,' I whispered, 'I've got it, you don't need to help me any more.'

I didn't know what to do, and I didn't know why he was holding on to me, why he was holding me against him, why he was pushing himself and the hard thing against my body. It wasn't fun, no matter that he told me otherwise. I was eager to please him, if only to stop the horrible things like being hit and having him swear at me, and I would also do anything to make Mum happy, but I had no idea what was happening. I didn't know why he was breathing so hard, why he was shoving himself into the back of my body over and over again. I didn't understand why he was making strange noises and why those noises suddenly stopped. Something happened – he made lots of funny little noises and his breath sounded as if he had just run up the stairs. All of a sudden, he stopped, let go of me and walked out of the room, only turning back at the door to state, 'That was fun.' Not a question, not a suggestion, just a bald fact in his mind and a clear instruction as to how I was supposed to process what had just happened. Left alone to finish making the bed, I dragged the duvet into place and struggled to stuff the pillows into the fresh cases, as I had seen Mum do before.

Within minutes, Gary arrived back. As I came out of Mum and Dad's room, I heard the front door open and the thud of his things landing on the floor. Dad looked at me and said, 'Remember – that was fun. You did well, Tracy, you did well.'

I was confused by so much, but I knew one thing – I knew *that* wasn't fun at all.

As Gary and Dad chatted as if nothing had happened, there was a knock at the door. I knew it couldn't be Mum, she wouldn't just arrive home, but it was the next best thing – Agnes.

'Just here to see if there's anything I can do, Harry,' she breezily announced, smiling at me. 'My offer still stands – why don't I take the kids? Valerie won't be back for a while, why don't you let me help out?'

I crossed my fingers behind my back and held my breath.

'No – I've told you, we don't need any help,' he snapped.

'Well, I'll just take Tracy then,' Agnes replied.

'No, no you will not. We don't need you. Anyway, I've got someone coming in to help.' With that, he slammed the door in her face and I saw my last chance disappear. I wanted to go with Agnes, but there was something else to cling on to. Dad had said that someone was coming to help out. This was quite a common occurrence with Army families – there were often offers of help if one of the mums was in hospital having a baby, or someone was ill. I had forgotten all about it until Dad snapped at Agnes.

'When is she coming, Dad?' I asked.

'What?' he barked. 'What are you talking about?'

'The lady who's coming to look after us – when will she be here?' I went on.

'You must be even more stupid than I thought!' he sniggered. 'I only said that to keep the interfering old cow out of my face. All you need to remember is this – clean up, shut up, and be a good girl.' And with that, I was sent to make dinner.

While the incident in the bedroom had been horrible, it had at least ended. The way Dad now spoke to me continued and it was unrelenting. He swore at me, shouted at me and hit me. With Mum in hospital, he gave me responsibility for household chores that were way beyond my years and capabilities. He got cross whenever I asked if Mum was coming home, or whether she was feeling any better. He wasn't like that with Gary at all. Their relationship continued along the same lines as always – it was my world that had been turned upside down. As the hours dragged on like days, I began noticing that any response he had to me fell into one of two categories. I was either a lazy bitch – *make dinner, clean the kitchen, vacuum this fucking carpet, shine my boots* – or a good girl. The 'good girl' comments were more general to begin with. Dad would shout at me, or rant that I should be doing something around the house in the absence of Mum, but then often imply that I would make him a lot happier if I was a 'good girl'.

I was only five, but I knew there was something wrong in this situation that went way beyond Mum being absent. Every time he told me that I was the 'woman of the house', my skin prickled with fear. Every time he said that I would have to try and be a good girl, without specifying what that entailed, a shiver ran through me as I thought of what had happened when we were changing the duvet cover. I just wanted Mum back; she had never been a warm, cuddly sort of mummy to me, but I wanted her there nonetheless.

I did all I could to please my dad and I tried to anticipate what might make him cross, so I would empty the ashtray which always seemed to be overflowing with his fag butts, and the old cardboard box which he threw his empty beer cans into. I did what I could to tidy up and clean things, and I was learning how to boil the kettle without burning myself, and make sandwiches without being too scared of the sharp knife. When Dad was visiting Mum in hospital, I did all of these chores, then sat on a chair, nervously awaiting his return. Gary was usually out playing, or at youth club, or football practice, but I had never been allowed these freedoms. He had always been treated differently by both our parents. I knew that Mum loved him more than she loved me; of course it hurt, but I accepted it, because it was just an obvious fact. She hugged him and kissed him, laughed when he was around, and always made sure he was warm, fed and happy. I was just an annoyance, and she had been telling me that for as long as I could remember, but it was strange that Dad treated us both so differently now too.

While Dad wasn't emotionally demonstrative with Gary, he was nevertheless more lenient with him. I was expected to stay at home, speak to no one and take on lots of responsibilities, whereas my brother's only rule was that if he had been sent outside to play, he wasn't allowed to come back in until Dad expressly told him to. There was to be no 'popping' back in if Dad and I were in the flat. Dad made it clear that there would be hell to pay if Gary came back early, or didn't wait until he was shouted on. My brother, like my mum, had never been particularly nice to me in my short life, but I was now wishing that he was around all of the time. I just felt that I wanted the presence of someone else; I didn't want to be alone with Dad at all.

By the time Mum had been in hospital for two nights, I felt as if she had been away for weeks. I was walking on eggshells, never sure of when Dad's mood would turn foul, and dreading that he might ask me to change the bedding again. It soon wasn't the only thing I learned to dread. 'Sit here beside me, Tracy,' he said on the third night, patting his chair in front of the TV after sending Gary off to bed early. I tried to perch on the edge but he pulled me in tightly towards him. 'You're a good girl, aren't you?' he said, ignoring the fact that I was flinching the whole time because we both knew that I had no choice but to be a good girl. 'Mum wants you to be a good girl, I want you to be a good girl too. Will you be a good girl for me, Tracy? Will you?'

I nodded, hating myself for agreeing because I associated being a good girl with the horror of his body pressing up against mine when we had changed the quilt.

'I hope you realise that good girls do what they're told, do you?'

Again, I nodded.

'Good girls make their daddies happy, don't they?'

He waited while I nodded again.

'Good girls enjoy the nice things that their daddies think of for them to do together – that makes their mummies happy too, doesn't it?'

I wasn't too sure about this because Mum was rarely happy unless it was as a result of something Gary did, but I nodded anyway, because I knew that was what was expected of me. I was so confused; I thought I was being a good girl, but I also had this sense that his idea of what that meant was very different to mine, even if I didn't know exactly what he wanted me to do. I didn't understand at all, but the fact that Dad kept going on about it made me think it must be important. When he first told me to be a good girl, there were so many other things that I hoped would tick that box – making a cup of tea, laying the table, changing the duvet cover. It soon became clear that there was one thing more than any other that made me 'good'.

'You're a good girl, and you worry about your mum, don't you?' Again, I nodded. 'You love your mum a lot, I know that – but what you need to know, Tracy, is that when she's ill . . . Well, that's often your fault. Did you know that, Tracy? That it's your fault?'

I felt so confused by all of this. I did love Mum, and I did want her to be well. I really didn't do anything to make her sick, I would never do that. I'm sure that Dad saw the confusion in my face.

'Your mum wants you to be good, and I want you to be good – because when you're good, that helps your mum to get better. Or . . .' he went on, 'it stops her getting ill in the first place.'

'I don't do anything bad, Dad, I really don't . . .' I started to say.

'Well, you don't fucking listen when I'm trying to explain things, do you?' he snapped. 'It's like this, Tracy – little girls need to be good for their mummies and their daddies. They listen to their daddies, and they make their daddies happy. And – are you listening as you should be? – when their daddies think of nice things for them to do together, they enjoy it. Hear me? They *enjoy* it. When good girls do that, everyone's happy.'

I sat there, on the chair, with the stench of him filling my nostrils. The beer and the cigarettes filled my senses, and all I could think was *I am good, I try to be, I really do.* I started to whisper it too.

He wasn't listening. He was talking, but he wasn't listening.

'There are other ways that little girls can be extra good . . .'

As he said this, he started to run his hands all over me, pushing my nightdress up. As I tried to pull it back down, his hand caught mine and stopped me from covering myself. I could see his face, it was contorted and ugly as he rubbed my body up and down, as he unzipped his trousers and started to touch himself, grunting, groaning, saying bad words to me.

The thing I remember most is that he kept saying I was *dirty*. I couldn't work that out either, but that night, after he touched me and said it over and over again, I thought I really must have been. His face became very red and he grunted for what seemed like such a long time, then he zipped up his trousers, pulled my nightie back down over my private parts and said harshly, 'Dirty little bitch like you needs to get a wash.'

Now I was desperate to go to bed, to fall asleep and forget the horror of him touching me, but his voice told me that I would not escape – not yet.

'Go to the bathroom and run a bath. Get in it and wait – don't close the door, don't lock the fucking door. You're filthy, absolutely fucking filthy, so get in there and wait for me.'

I did as I was told, shaking, not knowing what was going to happen. I feared that he would see me naked, and I was ashamed – even though he had touched me and seen things when my nightdress was pushed up, the thought of being completely naked in a bath was horrific.

He did look.

He stared and stared and stared at me as I sat in the water. I tried to wash myself as quickly as I could. I didn't do a very good job as I was so little, but he didn't seem to mind. There was no shouting, it was all quiet, but he couldn't take his eyes off me. I was scared to climb out on my own in case I slipped, but I didn't want to ask for help or hold my hand out for his, so I struggled on with everything, drying myself as best I could and putting on a clean pair of pyjamas. I looked at him as I walked past but he said nothing.

Lying in my bed, I wondered whether Dad would come into my room. Would he call me names, would he touch me again? I must have fallen asleep eventually on a pillow wet with tears. I wanted all of this to stop – and more than anything, I wanted Mum back home. That's all I ever really wanted: Mum.

CHAPTER 2

SUSPICIONS

Life fell into an awful pattern – but, as an Army child, patterns were something I was used to. It was frowned upon to step out of line at all as everything and everyone had a place. The base in Rinteln was like a little England. Even though we were Scottish (or at least Mum and Dad had been born in Scotland), it felt like home because we knew nothing else. All the Army homes seemed the same, and there were few personal possessions to make things more individual because people never knew when they'd been moving and they liked to travel light. We lived in a street which had three blocks of housing. In each of those blocks there were three homes. Every single home had the same layout and every other three-bedroomed house on the camp would be the same too.

The kids were expected to behave, as any naughtiness reflected on their parents, and physical punishment was rife. Other adults would shout at kids no matter whether they were theirs or not, but there was also a sense that we should all look out for each other, because, after all, our dads (and it was largely the men) were doing a job for Queen and country. The soldiers on the base were heroes, because everyone spoke of them that way, and I knew that, even though my dad only worked in an office and didn't fight, he was a hero too. He was very proud when he was in his uniform and he was always keen to look smart, with everything ironed and his boots well bulled. However, what the world didn't see was the man at home. The man who smoked constantly and threw the butts into an empty beer can, who drank all night without stopping, who stared at the TV with empty eyes. The man who would tell his five-year-old daughter to come and sit on the chair beside him at night when his wife was ill in hospital and his son had been sent to bed.

There were very clear roles for men and women. The wives and mothers were expected to keep the house clean, do the washing, make the meals, raise the kids – and most of them did. Some of them had part-time jobs, but this was only deemed acceptable if it didn't interfere with their 'real' jobs as wives and mothers. They all seemed to enjoy going to bingo, and they also liked selling parties, whether it was for Tupperware's plastic dishes or Pippa Dee's nylon clothes. It was a way for the women to get together without men or kids, giving them a chance to gossip about anyone who stepped out of line, or moan about their men. Although all of this was done within strict confines of what was accepted behaviour, it still gave them a chance to make friends quickly when they moved to a new base. Friendships were developed swiftly and mostly they were superficial – it was rare for people to stay in touch after moving – but the women helped each other out when they could. When Mum was ill or in hospital, Dad could have found plenty of people willing to help if he had let them, but he made it very clear that he wanted no such support. A man looking after his kids, struggling along in the absence of his ill wife, would have been seen as something of a saint. Only Agnes seemed to suspect anything; although Dad had rejected her numerous offers of help and tried to fob her off with the story about a woman coming in to help, Agnes continued in her attempts to get him to let her look after me.

Agnes and my mum had hit it off straight away when we arrived in Rinteln from Singapore. A few days after we first moved in to our house, she had knocked on our door while Dad was at the office. 'I'm your one-woman welcoming committee!' she announced with a smile as she waltzed in, carrying a tray on which there was a pot of tea, a jug of milk, a bowl of sugar and a plate of biscuits. She must have decided in advance that she would be there for a while, so had brought sufficient supplies for a full session of gossiping.

I wasn't at school at that point, so I sat on the floor, drawing on some sheets of scrap paper while the pair of them got to know each other.

'You'll like it here,' Agnes told Mum. 'There's a bingo hall, there are always Avon parties going on in someone's

house, and we all stick together. I've got a boy and a girl –
Roger and Denise – what about you?'

Mum waxed lyrical about Gary, who was at school, for a
while but Agnes came over beside me and crouched down
as I drew.

'Hello there, gorgeous,' she smiled – and I smiled back.
'What's your name?'

I shyly answered, 'Tracy,' and she ruffled my hair.

'Now, why aren't you at school?' she asked. 'A big girl
like you should be in class I'd think – what are you? Eight?
Nine?'

'I'm not at school! I'm only five!' I told her, pleased with
the idea that she had thought I was such a big girl. Mum
sat on the sofa with pursed lips, but Agnes stayed on the
floor with me, drawing a few stick men as she told me that
I'd have to meet her kids soon. I looked forward to it very
much, thinking that if the daughter was half as nice as she
was, she would be lovely.

The next day, Agnes came back again.

'Why don't I take Tracy to the park, Valerie?' she asked
Mum. 'Get her out in the fresh air, while you finish unpack-
ing the house?'

'I don't want to lumber you with this one, Agnes, she can
be quite a little madam. Are you sure it's no trouble?'

'No trouble at all, Valerie – we'll have a great time on the
swings. Would you like that, Tracy?' I nodded enthusiasti-
cally, and she took me by the hand as we headed out to the
playground. I had a lovely afternoon; from that moment on
Agnes became more like an auntie to me than a neighbour,

and I know that Mum always considered her a good friend too.

Agnes and her husband Graham were a bit older than Mum and Dad, maybe by about six or seven years. Denise was three years older than me, and Roger just a year or so. Gary and Denise wouldn't really lower themselves to play with me and Roger as we were too young for them to be seen with; it wouldn't have been 'cool'! However, I loved having anything to do with Denise as she was the type of girl I wanted to be, so even if she was just in the house when Mum and I went round to Agnes's, I would pretend that we were great friends and adore being in the same room as her.

Roger and I would play in the large communal garden together, sometimes with other kids. Our parents, mine and Roger's, could see us from the balconies of the flats if they wanted to. Often when I looked up, Mum wasn't there – when Gary was at school during the day, she didn't bother to check if I was OK or whether I needed any drinks or refreshments – but Agnes often sat on her balcony and watched us, often helping when we played hide and seek. She would also keep an eye out to stop the older kids bullying us. On a few occasions she would bring us down juice and biscuits. All the children liked her and I could see why. I remember one day a little girl asked me why my mum didn't give out treats, or even look for me. I shrugged and didn't answer, but Agnes was there and told them, 'Tracy's mummy is poorly.' She was often there to help out, and I longed for Mum to turn into a mummy just like her. This

33

happy time in my life lasted for a couple of months, until Mum was hospitalised and Dad put an end to any friendships I had made. He liked to keep me where he could see me, and make sure I told no one our secret. Sometimes when Roger came to ask if I could go out and play, Mum argued that my absence would give her 'peace and quiet', but Dad always said 'no' and stuck to his guns. Once or twice she let me go out to play if he wasn't there, but warned me never to let on.

Mum came home from hospital after a week or so. I wasn't told she was being released – I just came back from school one day, and she was there. Since she had been away, I had been left to walk to and from school alone each day. When I opened the door and caught a glimpse of her, my happiness just burst out of me.

'Mum!' I squealed, running towards her. The relief washed over me at the sight of her and I ran in her direction, desperate to be scooped up and hugged, desperate for some safety.

'Don't touch me!' she shouted before I was anywhere near her. 'Harry!' she shouted to Dad, who came out of the living room at her call. 'Keep her away from me – I'm just home, I don't want her pawing me and making me ill again. I've been in hospital, not away to the other side of the world. Now, give me some peace,' she said, turning back to me.

There was to be no emotional reunion. As hot tears welled in my eyes at her immediate rejection of me, something else hit me too. 'It'll be fine, Mum,' I said, making sure I was standing well away from her. 'You won't be ill again, I've been a good girl – haven't I, Dad?'

He sprung towards me from behind Mum.

'Leave your mum alone, come on, come with me,' he said, herding me towards my room.

'But—' I began.

'A good girl? You?' Mum laughed.

Dad pushed me roughly into my bedroom, calling to Mum that he would deal with me.

'Dad, I have been a good girl, I have . . .'

'No, no you haven't,' he whispered, threateningly. 'This is between us – we have to keep your mum well, but you can't go showing off about being good, Tracy. If you go bothering her, you'll make her ill again. She's not a well woman, and when you aren't good, it gets worse. And I will always know if you've been good enough, and you'll know it too, because if you haven't . . . she'll get sick again.'

He stood up and walked towards the door.

'Remember – it's up to you, Tracy, it's all up to you.'

That was it. That was the return of my mum. She batted me away without thinking, when I had done all I could to make her well. The confusion was overwhelming. I loved her so much and would have done anything for her, indeed I was doing all I could just as Dad had demanded, but she had no time for me, no time at all.

After a few weeks, Mum was back in hospital. Just as she had come home with no fanfare, she had been taken away again. This time, however, Dad wasted no time in telling me it was my fault.

'It's all down to you, of course,' he said, as he sat on his usual chair, drinking and chain-smoking even though it was only mid-afternoon.

'What is?' I whispered, fearfully.

'That the doctors have had to take your mum again,' he informed me.

'How?' I asked. 'What did I do?'

'For fuck's sake, Tracy!' he shouted. 'You know this! I told you that good girls need to do what their daddies tell them. If you're not good, then you have to expect . . . consequences.'

And off he went again, with the same warped rationale. Just as I had made Mum ill, I could also make her well again. If I wanted her back, if I wanted her to stop being sick, I had the power to make that happen. It was all down to me, all of it.

When you're naughty, it makes your Mum ill, Tracy.

When you don't do the things you should, she ends up in hospital.

When you are a good girl, she gets better.

Do you want her to be sick? Do you want her to be ill?

It's all up to you, Tracy – you can decide what happens.

Was that better or was that worse? Did I want to be the one who was in charge? Did I want to be the one who had all of the power?

No, I did not.

I wanted none of it.

I didn't want the things Dad did; I didn't want Mum to be ill. To be faced with the horrifying prospect that I had to allow the first to happen in order to avoid the second was more than I could comprehend. Dad told me it was all fine, he told me it was all normal – that these were fun things that all daddies did with their little girls. And, as he laid out the rules – *be good, do things, Mum will be fine* – he ran his hands all over my shaking body. As the tears ran down my face, I told myself the same thing over and over – I'm doing this for my mummy, I'm doing this for my mummy.

A few weeks after Mum came home after her hospitalisation on that stormy night, she went over to Agnes's for a cup of tea and a natter, and I went with her. By this time I lived in fear that if Mum ended up in hospital again, because I wasn't good enough, the things Dad was doing would get worse. He didn't touch me during this time of Mum being home, but I was too little to work things out – I didn't know when it would start again, I didn't know if he would do anything when Mum was in another room. All I did know was that, if she ended up being taken away again, it would be my fault and I would be punished.

I loved it at Agnes's house. It was just like ours in terms of layout and furniture, but much more friendly. It was bright and airy with nice, colourful soft furnishings. There were orange fluffy cushions on the settee and chairs and a couple of rugs to match the cushions. Agnes often had fresh flowers in the house, mainly pink carnations, and I always liked the way her house smelled. There were lots of photographs of her and her family, all in nice silver frames and in full view of anyone entering the sitting room. The photographs portrayed them as a very loving and close family, which they were. Agnes had made her house into a home, whereas ours was drab and devoid of happy pictures, which was no surprise really.

Mum and Agnes were busy talking about this and that, when Mum pushed back her chair and stood up. 'Oh, I've forgotten that magazine you were after!' she said.

'Which one?' asked Agnes.

'You know – the one that has the knitting pattern you wanted?' she replied.

She ran back upstairs to our flat to get the magazine. Agnes smiled at me as she stood up. 'Best pop the kettle on again before your Mum gets back,' she said, picking up the dirty mugs and walking through to the kitchen with them. The kitchen was attached to the living room, and I could see her as I played on the floor.

When the front door opened, I assumed it would be Mum coming back, but it was actually Agnes's husband, Graham. He went straight into the kitchen to where his wife was laying biscuits on a plate.

'What's she doing here?' he asked.

I heard Agnes mutter something before he continued.

'Tracy. That kid Tracy. Where's her mother? Where's Valerie?'

'She's just popped out to get me a magazine from their flat,' his wife said.

'I've told you before,' he snapped. 'They're funny buggers, her and her husband – I want them to stay away and I want you to make sure they stay away. I don't want them in my house.'

I didn't hear what Agnes said in reply, and I felt my ears were burning as this was surely something I shouldn't have been listening to. I'd always thought that Graham was a nice man – he would always say 'hello' to me or Gary when we saw him, often giving Gary a playful clout on the head as he passed by, as adults did in those days – but I didn't understand what he meant by 'funny buggers'. Did he mean me and my brother, or Mum and Dad, or all of us? And – more importantly – what had we done to make him think of us in that way?

As I was thinking all of this, Agnes came through to the sitting room, smiling at me.

'Are you all right, Tracy love?' she asked.

I nodded.

'Are you happy?' she went on.

'I like it here; I like your house,' I told her.

'That's nice – I like having you here; but are you happy when you're not here, Tracy?' she asked.

'What do you mean?' I queried.

'Well . . . you must be happy that your mum is well, but . . . are you happy in yourself, Tracy?' she said.

I could only focus on the main thing – yes, Mum was out of hospital so that meant, yes, I was happier than when she wasn't at home.

'Oh yes,' I beamed. 'I know Mummy is going to be OK now.'

'Do you, love? That's good. I hope so, I hope she is.'

But I knew. Agnes didn't have to hope, because I *knew*.

'She'll be fine because Daddy says that, as long as I'm a good girl, she won't go back to hospital. It's only when I'm

39

bad that that happens,' I told her, with the innocence of youth, forgetting Dad's warnings to say nothing.

Agnes looked quizzically at me.

'Of course you're a good girl,' she said, 'but Tracy, I wanted to ask you . . .'

She was interrupted at that point by the return of Mum, who handed the magazine over to her friend.

'I was just asking Tracy if she's happy to have you home and well, Valerie. It's a pity Harry wouldn't let her stay with me while you were in hospital. I'd take her any time, you know.'

'He didn't want to bother you, Agnes; and, well, you know what he's like – stubborn and independent,' replied Mum. 'Anyway, Tracy's hard work. She's a demanding little sod. I never get a minute's peace. She's not like Gary, he's no bother, but you'd be tearing your hair out with that one.'

Agnes smiled over to me.

'I think we'd get on just fine, wouldn't we, Tracy?' she asked, and I nodded, knowing that I would love to be with her if Mum did ever become unwell again. 'I wish Harry would think about it.'

'No – he's decided, so that's that,' said Mum.

They started chatting about this and that while I played on the rug, but something was still bothering me.

After a couple of minutes, I butted in and asked, 'Mum, what's a funny bugger?'

'A sorry bugger like you're going to be if I hear that again! Christ, Agnes – kids can't half embarrass you at times! Shut up and don't interrupt grown-ups,' she told me.

Agnes looked on, horrified, as she now knew that I had heard the conversation she'd had with her husband. My real question went unanswered and I knew that any further comment on the subject would be unwelcome – and I'd pay for it when we got home.

We left after Mum finished her coffee. As soon as we got home, she told Dad what had happened.

'Funny bugger, Harry! Asking what a funny bugger was! I tell you, I have never been so ashamed or so embarrassed in all my life. Where did she get that from?' she ranted.

Dad stared at me before speaking.

'It's that girl of Agnes's, I tell you, Valerie. Mouth like a sewer, that Denise has. I've heard her use foul language before,' he said, completely oblivious to his own hypocrisy, given the way he had recently begun swearing at me. He turned towards me before saying, 'She's a bad influence on you, Tracy, and I'm having none of it. You stay well away from her and stay out of the flat, you hear? And Val, you'd better keep away too and keep Agnes out of here, OK?'

'You're kidding, right?' Mum said. 'Agnes is my friend and she'll stay my friend – it's not my fault that this one is easily influenced, is it? I'll keep her away from Agnes, and her foul-mouthed daughter, and I'll try to keep Agnes away from here, but that's it.'

Mum did continue to go to see Agnes, although not as frequently, but it wouldn't be long before Dad banned Denise and Roger from the house, which made it clear to

Agnes that she wasn't really welcome either. However, although I wasn't allowed back to Agnes's house, this didn't go for Gary; he was still allowed to visit. It wasn't fair, but I knew there was no point in complaining. Dad had what he wanted – a valid reason, in his mind and in Mum's, for keeping me away from Agnes, and to stop her coming round. I had done nothing but make things worse for myself.

Over the next six months, Mum was in and out of hospital a lot. The doctors were still baffled, and I was still just as confused, albeit for different reasons. I was trying so hard to be good, but she was still being taken away. What was I doing wrong? What more could I do?

Each time she left, Dad would make his theories very clear to me.

'This is your fault, Tracy, your fault.'

I would hang my head because, the truth is, I couldn't help but believe him. Mum did keep getting ill and something was causing it. If my Dad said I was the problem, then how could I possibly argue?

But I was so confused. Confused and terrified. I didn't want to do the things that I knew made me 'good' but I *had* been doing them and it was still all going wrong. I had to be brave enough to ask – I had to be brave enough to ask Dad why it wasn't working.

'What am I doing wrong, Dad?' I whispered.

'What do you mean?'

'I'm trying to be good, but Mum's still ill – what am I doing wrong?'

'You're not trying bloody hard enough!' he snapped. 'You're the woman of the house now – even when your mum's here she's not well enough to be doing everything. She can do a bit of cleaning, a bit of cooking, but there are other things you'll have to do.'

I could feel his eyes staring into my soul. He was my dad, he had to be telling the truth, he had to be looking out for me; that's what dads did. I was just a five-year-old girl who was naughty, how could I challenge anything?

'You need to remember that this is all for your mum, Tracy – these are good things, you can enjoy it when we have fun together . . . it's all good . . .'

Then it would all start. He would touch me in places that I knew were private, and he would look at my naked body in ways that I hated. He would start to breathe strangely as he looked at me, and touched me, and he would push against me with his own body.

'You can be a good girl or a bad girl, Tracy – that's what you are, isn't it?' he would say, as he panted. 'You're a good girl. You're a dirty little bitch. You're a good girl. You're a dirty little bitch.' It was as if he was chanting those words, and I couldn't make head nor tail of it. How could I be both? Being dirty was bad, not good, and I wasn't dirty anyway – he was always making me have a bath.

As he said it over and over again, I would feel that strange, lumpy thing in his trousers. We didn't see sex on the telly all the time back then, there was nothing around us which constantly suggested sex or sexualised children. I didn't have words for what was happening, but I felt

43

ashamed. I was also utterly baffled about why, if I was a good girl when all of this was going on, he called me such horrible names. *Good girl, dirty little bitch, good girl, dirty little bitch.* How could I be good and dirty at the same time? How could I be good and a bitch? How could I be good and filthy? This bothered me all the time.

But I couldn't ask anyone to explain it. I couldn't ask Mum what was going on, because Dad would constantly remind me to keep quiet.

'No blabbing,' he'd hiss if Mum was in the house while he touched me. 'Remember – this is between us, or it doesn't work.' I did as I was told, even if I was mystified by it all. I would have done anything for Mum, anything at all – and I did. It didn't matter that she barely looked at me, that she hardly ever showed me any affection, she was my mum, and there is something so special, so precious about that relationship that it defies all logic, even when the child in the middle of it is having their heart broken.

He was a very clever man. Abusers generally are. He took the very thing that would drive me to do anything and used it for his own perversions. At that age, I had no idea that he could, often, predict the worsening of Mum's symptoms. He could see when she was working up towards another stay in hospital, and he would tell me that I'd better enjoy the fun he had planned, because she was getting worse again and he suspected she would be taken away soon. And sure enough, as her health would begin to deteriorate again, she would say to Dad when he came in from work, 'I've had a terrible day, Harry. This one . . .' she'd point at me, 'this one just *drains* me. She bothers me from first thing in the morning, you have no idea. She follows me round like a dog, she just hangs on to me and it is doing nothing for my health, nothing at all.' Dad would look at me, shake his head and walk past. But later, when we were alone, he would ask me, 'Have you any idea how hard you're making things for everyone? Mum's health is in your hands and if you want to keep her out of hospital, you have to be a good girl.'

Their conversations were always the same – Mum would complain about me, and Dad would use her complaints to control me. It was only as I got older and became more aware of how relationships seemed to work between other people's parents that I realised that my parents never seemed to have any 'banter' going on between them. There was very little that was light-hearted. If they hadn't had me to complain about to each other, I'm not sure that Mum and Dad would ever have spoken. 'It's not normal, Harry!' Mum would often shout. 'It's not normal for a child to be such hard work!'

In fact, I *was* just a normal little girl who wanted her mummy. I didn't drain her, I didn't ask her for more than any child would; in fact, I did lots of things for myself, but I suppose her illness did make her tired so perhaps the normal demands of being a parent weighed more heavily on her. However, she always made it seem as if I was being particularly demanding, indeed, *maliciously* demanding. If I wanted something to drink or eat, she'd sigh and say 'Again?' as if I was constantly asking for things – even if it was hours after mealtime and she'd forgotten to feed me anyway. If I went to take something for myself, she'd slap my hand away and tell me to stop being so greedy. I couldn't win. Dad had said I was the woman of the house and that I needed to make meals, do the cleaning, and generally take the place of his wife, but when I did these things in the presence of Mum, she'd shout me down, then go on to tell Dad how awful I was when he got home. If I asked her to do things for me, as any little girl would, again, I was 'constantly' wanting 'everything'. If I tried to hug her or kiss her, she'd flap her hands at me and say she couldn't get a minute's peace without me 'mauling' her.

I may know now that she never loved me, but back then I still had hope. I was only five years old and all children at that age cling on to hope – they hope that Christmas will come quickly, they hope they'll get a new bike for their birthday, they hope the Tooth Fairy will leave some money under their pillow. I hoped Dad would stop abusing me and Mum would get better. If I'd had to make a choice between those two things at that stage, I would have chosen Mum every time. I did choose her every time. Given that I could see she was capable of love, she was capable of being a good mum – I knew she could, because I saw her being a good mum to Gary – I reckoned that I just had to work out how to become the sort of little girl she wanted. Every time Dad touched me, I thought, *I'm doing this for Mum.* Every time he told me to take my clothes off, I thought,

46

This will make Mum better. Every time he pushed himself against me and grunted, I thought, *This is helping more than anything the doctors can do.* And every time he leered at me as I scrubbed at my body the way he liked, I thought, *This will stop Mum being sick.*

CHAPTER 3

ALL MY FAULT

I felt so alone and removed from the world around me –
and Dad was doing all he could to encourage that. Once,
when he was watching me in the bath, not long after the
abuse had started, he said: 'Just remember – no fucker
wants you. Nobody wants to look after you and nobody
cares.' He would often tell me these things.

No one wants you.

No one cares for you.

No one loves you.

And then would come the words I hated most.

Apart from me.

I want you.

I care for you.

I love you.

Remember that.

Understand that.

Never forget that.

Of course I wanted love – but not that kind of love, not the twisted version he offered me that I could never refuse.

It became a pattern. First of all, he'd tell me that there was no one there for me. Then he'd tell me that he was the only exception, that he was all I had. Then he would say, *Remember that, never forget it, listen to me, do you hear me?* And I had to agree, I had to nod, and I had to fight so hard from screaming.

Of course, there were some happy times, even if there was always a feeling that I was the outsider. The abuse didn't happen every day, it wasn't constant – and sometimes I could pretend for a few hours that ours was a normal family, one that did normal things.

I always tried to get some enjoyment out of things when I could. This was partly because I was still so young and partly because the bad stuff needed to be pushed away. So, when I was about six, I was really excited when I heard my parents talk in the kitchen about ballet lessons.

I paused outside the door when I heard the word 'ballet' and felt a thrill that this might be something that could happen.

'All the other women send their daughters to the classes,' I could hear Mum say. 'Why should I be any different? Why shouldn't I get what I want?'

'She doesn't need bloody ballet lessons,' grumbled Dad. 'She doesn't need to be mixing with other children, getting leered at in a little skirt and prancing about.'

'So, I get left out again?' moaned Mum.

'Just leave it, Valerie,' said Dad.

'No – no, I bloody won't leave it,' she said. 'It's normal, all the other women send their girls, why should I be denied? As if it isn't enough that I'm ill, as if that isn't enough!'

For once, her selfishness worked in my favour and Dad relented. On Fridays, after school, I arrived at the gym hall where the classes were held. I loved it from the moment I started.

On the first day, Mum had put a tiny black leotard and pink block shoes into my school bag. There was always someone on the base growing out of their things, so they tended to get passed around. I wasn't bothered about missing out on the excitement of going shopping for new things because I was just so thrilled that I was being given the opportunity at all. I knew Dad wasn't happy about it all, but his only comment the previous evening had been a whispered, 'Mind – don't go getting too friendly with anyone; don't go telling them your business.' I did as I was told, I kept myself to myself, and I practised every spare minute of the day.

One day, after I had been going for about six weeks, I was in the hall at home. Our ballet teacher had said that we needed to do as many exercises as we could at home, and that this was particularly important for the splits. She told us all that we needed to get bendier and stretchier, and that we just needed to move a little more every time, then, one day, it would happen.

I had my leotard and pink shoes on, and my most determined face. Mum was in the kitchen having a cup of tea and a gossip with her friend, Diane. Diane was Mum's only confidante at this time; Dad was becomingly increasingly negative towards Agnes, but Diane was still allowed in the house and she visited Mum in hospital a fair bit too. Dad wasn't at home, so I had relaxed a little. I didn't like him to see me in my ballet clothes – I wanted to keep all of that for me, away from the nasty things he did, and away from the funny looks he gave me.

I could hear Mum and Diane chatting, and I proudly bent and stretched, trying to remember what the teacher had said. I thought I was the bee's knees, twirling around as if I was in *Swan Lake*!

'What are you up to out there?' shouted Mum.

'Doing my ballet, I'm practising my splits!' I called back, proud of myself.

I could hear them laughing at me, but it felt nice. It was so rare to have any positive attention from Mum, although she was always a bit better with an audience anyway.

'Come on, then!' she replied. 'Come through to the kitchen and show us how good you are.'

I trotted through immediately, delighted that she was showing an interest, even if it was for Diane's benefit. I began to lower myself onto the kitchen floor, only able to get down so far, as I was still a beginner. Mum was standing behind me as I tried, and she was commentating all the time.

'Get right down, Tracy!' she shouted. 'Try a bit harder! Don't show me up – you said you could do the splits, but I can't see you managing!'

'I'm trying my hardest, Mum,' I said. 'I can't get all the way down yet, I've got to keep practising.'

Mum snorted dismissively.

'Aw, bless her, Valerie,' said Diane. 'You're doing brilliantly, love — well done, you're a regular little ballerina, aren't you?'

I was about five inches from the floor when suddenly I felt a searing pain. I thought I was going to split in two, and it took me what seemed like ages before I realised what was happening. Mum had her hands on my shoulders and was pushing me all the way down to the floor. I began screaming due to the pain, but Mum just stood there laughing, holding me in place and shoving me as hard as she could. I swear I could hear a cracking noise as I was pushed more and more, and my legs opened wider and wider.

'Well, you can do them now!' she giggled, as if it was all great fun. 'Remember what your dad says — nothing's worth doing unless you do it right.'

She had released me by this point but I was still on the floor, crying in pain. It was Diane, not my mum, who picked me up and gave me a cuddle.

'You poor thing,' she said, consolingly. 'It'll be fine, you just got a fright. What were you thinking of, Val? You could have really hurt her there.'

Mum couldn't have cared less. She should have been the one consoling me — well, she should never have hurt me in the first place — but it was Diane who cared, Diane who realised what had happened.

Mum turned her back on both of us and filled the kettle.

'God, what a baby!' she exclaimed. 'It's a good job your father isn't here, Tracy.' She paused for a second. 'What time are we going to the bingo tonight, Diane?' she asked, as if nothing had happened.

Diane sat on the floor with me, cuddling me until my crying subsided.

'Are you all right, love?' she asked.

I nodded, and she patted my back as I stood up.

'Go on and get dressed,' said Mum. 'That's enough drama for the day. You've caused a big enough scene. The ballet lesson is now finished!' she declared in a booming voice, as if it had all been terribly funny.

I went to my room and heard Diane leave after a while. She called, 'Bye, Tracy!' as she went out, and I waited to see if Mum would start shouting at me. Surprisingly, she didn't, but as soon as she heard Dad's key in the lock about an hour later, all hell broke loose.

'Harry! Harry! Come here!' she shouted.

'What's wrong?' he yelled back, rushing into their bedroom where she was waiting. 'Are you ill again, Valerie?'

'I bloody will be if that little madam gets her way!' I heard her say. Within seconds, she and Dad were at my bedroom door and Mum was pointing her finger at me accusingly.

'Tell him – tell him what you got up to today,' she said, but before I could say a word, she had launched into her own version of events. 'Diane was here for a cup of tea but madam there couldn't leave us be, she had to get all the attention.' She nodded at me, as if to say, *that's what happened, that's what went on.* 'She was back and forwards all bloody afternoon – ballet this, and ballet that, watch me do this, watch me do that. I tell you, Harry, she'll be the death of me.'

'Is this true? Have you been bothering your mother when she just wants a bit of peace?' asked Dad.

I shook my head, but Mum was off again.

'Oh, she'll lie till she's blue in the face, that one, she'll swear black is white. You're right, Harry, she's not to be trusted.'

What had he been saying? I wondered. *What had he been saying about not trusting me if I said things?*

'Anyway, in she comes, just when I was trying to have a nice quiet afternoon. "Watch me doing the splits," she says, and, of course, Diane's too polite to ignore her . . .'

'She needs bloody ignoring,' said Dad as Mum nodded in agreement.

'. . . and then, before I knew what was happening, she was wailing like a fucking banshee! Claiming that she'd hurt herself, claiming that she was split in two. I tell you, Harry, she's an attention-seeker all right.'

They both stood looking at me, perfectly happy with their own lies.

'Well, it's obvious to me what we need to do,' said Dad. 'The ballet classes need to stop.'

Mum smiled triumphantly. 'If you think so, Harry, if you think so.'

'No, Dad, please no!' I pleaded.

'It's been decided, Tracy. You have to face up to the consequences of your behaviour. Now go to bed; no dinner for you tonight.'

As Mum left the room, happy with what she had achieved, he looked back at me before the door was fully closed. 'Do NOT draw attention to yourself,' he said. 'Is this really the way a good girl would behave? I wouldn't be at all surprised if this pushed your mother into sickness again. I can only hope that you find a way to make it all better, Tracy, I really do.'

There were always those threats. Whatever I did, there was always a way he could link it to the ways in which he would exercise control over me. He always wanted the same thing, and he always managed to find a way to remind me what that was. In the middle of it all, Mum's lack of affection hit me hard. It was as if she stuck the knife in whenever she could.

As time went on, the awful duality of my existence weighed even heavier upon me. Dad's abuses were increasing, and Mum was still getting ill. I was always confused. I had to find one truth in the middle of it all, and I had to hold on to what I desperately needed to believe – these things happened to all little girls with ill mummies, and I was doing all I could to prevent my own mum from getting any worse, so I simply had to endure it. When Dad was abusing me, he would say afterwards that he could 'only hope that enough has been done'. There was always the implication that I could have done more, or that I could have offered myself up to be abused more easily, or that I could have acted more willingly. When he told me to get in the bath, he would look at me so coldly and with such hatred as his eyes flicked over me that I always felt I had done badly, and the shame which coursed through my body added to my self-hatred.

I do feel that Dad knew what he was doing because, from a very early stage, he would try to justify himself to me, and convince me that his actions were the right ones. If he hadn't known what he was doing, or couldn't control himself in some way, then why would he have done that? On one occasion, when Mum was in hospital again and after the abuse had happened that night, Dad didn't send me for a bath. This was completely out of character. As I lay on the bed shaking, with him lying beside me, he asked if I was all right. I don't think he wanted a truthful answer. In fact, I don't think he wanted an answer at all as he started to justify himself yet again.

'I'm a good dad, you know, Tracy,' he said. 'I'm bringing you up. I'm bringing Gary up. It isn't easy, it isn't easy at all. Your mother's never out of that bloody hospital and here I am, holding down an important job and raising two kids on my own. I'm a good dad, I am; everyone says so.'

I was six years old. My life was one in which abuse had been completely normalised by the man who was keen to tell me what a good father he was as I lay naked beside him, terrified as I dealt with the aftermath of his abuse of me. I never knew when he would hit me, I never knew when he would touch me, but I did know that it was all completely in his power. He would swear at me pretty much all the time and make me take on household duties way beyond my years. He gave Gary money constantly, to keep him out of the house so that his abuse of me could take place uninterrupted.

What a good dad.

Mum was either absent or cold to me; Gary only made fun of the little sister he knew was disliked by the woman who adored him; I had no friends, no other family nearby, and I wasn't allowed near Agnes because of Denise's 'influence'. The only affection I got was from the man who was abusing me. Dad had started to use some affectionate terms now, too, rather than just the usual bad names. Words like 'doll' and 'sweetheart'. He told me that he loved me and he gave me cuddles and he said I was good when I did the things he wanted. No one else did that. I had no idea how to react – was he saying these things for me or for him? Sickeningly, was he trying to convince himself that we had a 'real' relationship, that I had taken the place of his wife, and that if he thought of the right words, the right caresses, it would all be fine? It turns my stomach to even think that, but sometimes I do feel that was his mind-set.

As time went on, and Mum's hospitalisations became a fact of life, I was becoming more and more uncared for. I wanted Dad to stop doing those things to me – that goes without saying, because I didn't know how much more I could stand of it – but I wanted everything else to go back to normal too. I wanted Mum to get better, because I loved her and I couldn't think of anything I could do to help more. But I also wanted her back to do the practical things, because I simply couldn't cope with running a house when I was still so little – I ended up doing everything badly and getting battered for it, I never ate properly or wore fresh clothes. Dad took his own laundry to the Mess, but I was left with the task of washing everything else, loading it into a twin tub, drying it – and generally making a real pig's ear of the whole job. I couldn't carry the piles of wet clothing and I had no idea how to dry it all properly, so I ended up with clothes which smelled damp and mouldy, probably worse than they would have done if I hadn't been told to wash them in the first place. I didn't linger in the bath. If Dad was watching me, I wanted out as quickly as possible; if he wasn't there, I rushed in case he did come in. Whether I was alone in there or not, the result was the same – I was filthy. My long hair was rarely shampooed and I couldn't brush it properly as it was so long. It soon became matted and was something else to mark me as different from other little girls. Mum must have noticed the state I was in, yet she would make no comment when she returned from her most recent hospitalisation. Perhaps she felt she didn't have the energy to think about it, or perhaps she didn't want to ask Dad why he hadn't been looking after me properly in case it meant acknowledging other failings of his conduct as a father. Whatever the reason, it all boiled down to the fact that she just didn't care. I have often wondered, in retrospect, whether all of this was part of my dad's plan to make me even more sepa-rate from the other kids. They soon noticed the stink coming from me, with the result that I had no real friends, no one to confide in.

The children at school largely avoided me. I had an air of neglect about me and there was one girl, Erin, who was eight, and two years above me. She had taken to calling me 'smelly' whenever she could. She also called me a 'tramp', which was one of the words Dad would use, and, in my confused state, I would often get upset at the thought of whether or not she knew what was happening behind closed doors. Erin called me hurtful names whenever she saw me. She was just one of those girls who had a talent for identifying the weakest of the pack and exploiting that weakness.

One day, on the way home from school, Erin was calling me names as usual, and I just flipped. I couldn't take any more, so I pushed her as hard as I could. She turned around instantly and we started to fight. I had bitten off more than I could chew; she absolutely leathered me. I went home, crying and bleeding.

'What's happened to you?' asked Mum. When I told her, the immediate response was, 'So, she beat you?'

I nodded, waiting for some consolation. I was stunned when all I got was a slap.

'You listen to me,' she said. 'Get back out there and find that little cow! Find her and give her a good thumping – do you hear me?'

There was no point in arguing. I'd just get another slap, so off I went, back into the street to see if I could track Erin down. She was sitting on a wall a few hundred metres away, looking miserable.

'What the fuck do you want, smelly?' she asked, aggressively.

'Nothing,' I lied.

'Piss off then,' she responded.

I didn't, so after a few moments, she asked again.

'My mum says I've to find you and give you a hammering,' I told her, quietly. I didn't have the bravado required; I knew Erin could easily beat me in a fight.

'Did she now? She must be as stupid as my mother then. Come here, stinky,' she said, patting the wall beside her. 'Maybe if we both sit here long enough, they'll have got a bit cleverer by the time we get back.'

Erin and I chatted for a while that day. I wouldn't say we became friends, but by the time we both made our way home we had certainly made a sort of peace with each other. We never fought again. She still called me names, but less often and with less enthusiasm. She never did tell me what was wrong with her home life, but there was clearly something going on there that made her act the way she did. When I got home, Mum snapped, 'Did you sort her out?' I nodded. She held my face up to the light, exposing the cuts and marks from the first run-in, and seemed satisfied.

'Good,' she said. 'Good.'

That was the closest I ever got to support.

I wanted everything to go back to normal, for something to break this horrific pattern of abuse, beatings and neglect. I prayed for it all to stop, for something to change. Then, one day, it seemed as if my prayers had been answered: Gary and I were told that we were moving to Northern Ireland. A new house, a new life, new people. At last, I saw that maybe things would be different. New doctors would possibly work out what was wrong with Mum, and if she was healthy I wouldn't have to try to keep her that way by doing what Dad wanted. A new school could mean teachers who saw that I was unhappy and who did something about it. A new house in a new area could mean new friends for all of us, and that could mean all manner of possibilities. For the first time in as long as I could remember, I went to bed with hope in my heart. We were moving and there was a chance that it could all be different.

CHAPTER 4

CAMPING

There was nothing different about the set-up in Northern Ireland, apart from the threat of violence outside the camp. We were all given warnings about not trusting anyone, about being constantly alert, about staying in the camp whenever possible. The actual accommodation was identical to everywhere else, same furniture, same layout. The school was only about one hundred metres away from home, which meant I could walk there and back, but there were plenty of other restrictions, both in terms of Army and home life. The political situation was one we were all aware of, no matter how young. The 1970s were a bad time to be in Northern Ireland if you were military or police, and no one ever really knew if their husband or father would come home from work each day.

Nothing was different with Mum, either, despite the move. She would constantly say I was a 'fucking nuisance' and 'a pain in the arse'. She had a list of complaints that she would reel off to anyone who would listen, loud enough so that I would hear. I was draining the life out of her. I was making her life a misery. I'd be the death of her. All of these comments simply emphasised what I already feared – her illness was my fault. It was all down to me. If I hurt myself and asked for a plaster, I was demanding. If I cried, I was a drama queen. If I tried to hug her, I was a leech. If I kept myself to myself, I was cold and not interested in how she was feeling.

Before we moved to Northern Ireland, Mum had already become more dependent on Dad, as she could never tell when she would get ill. So Dad was more confident in hitting me in front of her – and she was slapping me about a fair bit too – as well as swearing at me. Whereas she would never have allowed this before the abuse began, she let everything slip now and I was always at the mercy of one or the other of them. Dad also grew more confident in his abuse of me. He started touching me whenever the opportunity arose, and now he was also making me touch him. When he had first forced me to masturbate him, he had seemed shocked when the wetness appeared and told me that I was 'fucking disgusting' for having 'that stuff' on my hand. It quickly became an ordinary event for him, however. He would drop his trousers and pants, take *that* out and get me to touch it while he said horrible things to me, telling me that I loved it, on a regular basis. I felt as if I smelled of him all the time, I smelled of his touch.

We had arrived in Northern Ireland as the Troubles were intensifying, and the Army was trying to repair relations with the community. It was a losing battle, as anyone with the slightest bit of historical knowledge will be aware, but they did make some attempts. It was as if the political problems and riots could all be papered over with some effective public relations talk and a few 'inclusive' events. We had already been living in Northern Ireland for about a year when it was announced that a camping trip was to be arranged to bring together kids on the base with a group of orphaned Irish children of similar ages. I suppose the thinking behind it was that perhaps children could build bridges in a way that adults couldn't, but that sort of belief was seriously flawed. Not only was every child on that base raised on stories of how dangerous their fathers' jobs were, but the local children were similarly raised to hate us and everything we stood for. As soon as we heard about it, most of the kids thought it would be an unmitigated disaster – there was too much bad blood on both sides.

There had been rumours going round school about the holiday, but I was told of the trip 'officially' one afternoon when I got in from school. I was nine, and the idea of a holiday was completely alien to me – as an Army child, holidays didn't feature much in my life. We had moved around a bit, and we certainly didn't have a traditional, happy mum-dad-and-the-kids setup, so two weeks away every summer would have just been a bit too normal for us. On top of that, it was difficult to predict when Mum would be in hospital or how ill she would be.

'You're going camping,' Mum said to me brusquely when I went into the living room. She was dusting her little ornaments and Avon trinkets – they were her pride and joy in our otherwise cold and drab home, and always something which engaged her much more than any conversation with me. It made her happy, and she loved to potter about with her collections, which made the journey from house to house, base to base.

'When? Where?' I asked.

'Couple of weeks – couple of hours away,' she replied, continuing to dust, then moving on to the ironing as she spoke. 'It's an Army thing. You're going with other kids, Irish ones as well. You've to bond. Gary's going too.'

I wasn't sure what to think – I didn't want to go, and I couldn't see why she would let me do something that might appear to be fun. She preferred me to be miserable, as I fitted into her idea of who the real Tracy was when I was like that. I wasn't usually allowed to be with other children, and I had no idea what was meant by 'bonding'. Gary was already jumping around, excited by the idea and determined to have a good time.

'It'll be brilliant!' he shouted.

'Oooh, I hope you're going to miss me though?' said Mum, hugging him to her.

'Sure,' he said, dismissively. 'Camping! Camping! I'm going camping!'

'I don't really want to go camping,' I told her. Although I hated my life at home, I didn't want to go away either, to some unknown place, into some unknown situation, with lots of people I didn't know. I'd never been camping before and I had no desperate desire to begin.

'Tough,' my mum said, the smile on her face disappearing as soon as she looked at me. 'You're going – I'll get a break, if nothing else. I can tell you one thing – getting rid of you hanging round me will be like a holiday for me as well, so I couldn't really care less what you want.'

I knew better than to argue, or even ask any more questions at that point. Mum was already no doubt fantasising about how much bingo she was going to fit in while we were away, and I would be shouted at even more if I interrupted those daydreams. She went back to the ironing, Gary continued to jump about, and I went to my room, working out how I could escape the 'adventure'.

From that point, it seemed that everyone was talking about the trip. The place we were going to was actually about three hours from the base, and the holiday itself was to be for only three days – we'd leave on the Friday at 7 a.m. and return late on Sunday evening.

The religious aspect was certainly flogged to death. Whatever God we believed in wouldn't matter, nationality wouldn't matter, politics wouldn't matter. We'd just be a group of happy little children all playing together without a care in the world. To some extent, some people did subscribe to it. I may not have had many friends, due to my dad controlling my movements so much, but I often watched others and I could see how they, like the wives on the bases, would make friends easily. My brother would simply start playing football with a group of boys, even if he didn't know them, and before long they would be his 'best mates', at least until one of them moved again. So I did think it might be how 'normal' kids worked.

As the date for going on the trip got closer, I started to wonder whether it might be all right, but I wasn't sure what to expect. One day, after school, while I was pondering this, Dad interrupted my thoughts.

'You looking forward to the trip?' he asked.

'Sort of,' I said, wary of committing myself.

'I am,' he replied.

I knew that Mum would be glad to get rid of me, but I didn't know that both my parents felt the same way.

'I'm looking forward to coming on the trip,' he said with a smile on his face, as it all registered with me.

Until that point, I had no idea that he would be going too and, from that moment, I was terrified. There were to be about forty children there, with only a dozen or so from Army families. Their ages would range from the same as me, about nine, to teenagers. There would also be a batch of adults, all Army men of different ranks who were assigned six kids each. There were no women there, and this worried me hugely. I had always felt safer with women around. Mum might not be perfect, but she had never come close to doing things as bad as those inflicted on me by Dad. She preferred emotional abuse. I still thought warmly of Agnes, and there had never been

any woman in my life who had touched me inappropri-
ately or made me do things to her. The idea of a camping
trip with no women there was awful. I knew that the
other kids, the non-Army ones, were orphans, but I had
still assumed that some of the Army wives would be
there. Now, I was faced with a trip just with Dad and lots
of other men – men who could be, potentially, just like
him.

'You're going?' I whispered.

'Of course,' he said. 'I've been chosen – selected. I'm not
doing it for you and Gary,' he emphasised. 'I'm doing it for
my rank. This is important – a chance for me to be seen to
be doing my job, doing it well, so don't you dare let me
down, you hear?'

I didn't care why he was going – I just knew that I didn't
want him to. Once I knew that he would be there as well, I
was terrified. This was nothing to do with the Army or
religion or politics, it was nothing to do with bonding or
making orphaned kids feel better, it was about abusing me,
I was sure of it. I couldn't think of anything else, I couldn't
get another thought into my head. I truly believed that he
was taking me away from Mum to abuse me even more. I
also thought that all the other kids were in the same boat
as me; there were even orphans there who had, presumably,
been so bad that their mums had died, so they had even less
chance of being protected (not that my own mother did
much to protect me). Dad was always building up the pressure, constantly saying that Mum's illness was my fault
and that it was my choice whether she was in pain or

hospitalised. He was also trying to normalise my abuse by saying that this was just something which happened, that lots of little girls did these things with their daddies. Was that the real reason behind the trip, I wondered? Were they trying to get all of us together to do 'bad' things? Were there a lot of mums who needed saving, or was it just to impress upon us that we needed to do as we were told or there would be consequences?

What should have been an exciting time for me was really very scary. I was so apprehensive that my stomach was in knots constantly. Even though we knew the reasoning behind it and had discussed it in school, I was convinced it was a trick.

One day, when Dad was still at work and we were on our own together, I tried again to tell Mum that I didn't want to go and would rather stay at home with her.

'Don't be so bloody stupid!' she shouted. 'You're going! I need the rest, I never get one of those while you're in the bloody house. Christ, all that's been keeping me going is the thought of getting a break from you for a while – I'll bloody scream if that gets taken away from me. Really? Really, Tracy? You would take this away from your own mother? After all you do to me, you would take this tiny, tiny bit of pleasure from me? You must know how much I'm sacrificing, you must know how much I'll miss my Gary, but still you only think of yourself. God only knows what I've done to deserve you!'

As usual, it was all about her.

But I kept trying. I had to – this was taking on such monstrous proportions in my head that I was even willing to risk her wrath.

'Mum,' I went on, trying to stay calm and reasonable but knowing she'd fly off the handle very soon, 'I can stay and spend the time looking after you just in case you get ill again.'

'I won't get ill; I'll be a lot better if I get a rest from you. Anyway, what could you do if I did? You're better off going, in fact I'm looking forward to having the place to myself without you lot, especially you,' she replied.

I couldn't let it go. I was so worried that I was being sent into a trap, and I wanted her to save me – at least this one time.

'But Mum, it's all daddies there – no mummies are going!'

'So? Now they'll see what shit we have to put up with you pain-in-the-arse kids. You and your brother are going. That's final. OK?'

I didn't want it to be final, I didn't want to hear the word 'no', so I left it for five minutes then tried again using a different ploy.

'Mum, I don't know all the people on the trip and I'm scared. Can't I stay here with you? Please?' I begged.

'Oh, bloody hell! Stay in case I get ill or because you're scared? Make up your mind about your excuse, but if you keep it up, you're going to make me ill. I've decided, so shut up. Piss off and leave me alone, do you want your dad to know you're pestering me?'

Dad finding out was the last thing I wanted so I kept quiet and didn't push it any further. She wasn't even concerned enough to ask why I was scared.

Looking back, she had a cheek. She was hardly ever there, so the notion that she needed some peace and quiet, especially where I was concerned, was a joke. She never really had anything to do with me anyway, Dad made sure of that. She may have cooked and cleaned when she was able, but she never really 'looked after' me. Gary was the only one she had time for, and I bet if he had asked to stay at home, she would have been fine with that. What hurt most was this feeling I had that I was being sent into danger; the realisation that she wasn't trying to protect me from it fell like a hammer blow.

The dreaded weekend soon came around, and early on the Friday morning we were packed into minibuses and driven to the campsite. The journey was torture for me, as I ran through in my head all the possible bad things that might happen when we got there. By the time we arrived, I was a nervous wreck. We were told that we had to set our own tents up. There were lines of tents for the girls on one side, with the boys on the other, and the adults in the middle. As we started putting them up, some of my fear began to subside – it was actually quite fun, although we needed help from the grown-ups, and I was surprised that I did enjoy myself so early on. We all had army-issue sleeping bags and were given a list of activities we could access while on the trip, including pony trekking, orien-teering, paper chase, tug-of-war, and singing around the camp fire in the evenings. The adults took turns in cooking, although the kids helped prepare some of the food. Most of it was army-issue compo food. These tins were gold-coloured and the contents were labelled on the top of the tin in black. Dad often brought these tins home for the three of us when Mum was hospitalised; they usually contained foods such as processed cheese, stewed steak, beans, sausages and mince, and the ones that the kids really liked were the ones with boiled sweets or chocolate.

Although I remained apprehensive throughout the trip, I attached myself to an older Irish girl, Deborah, who was about thirteen. Where Deborah went I followed, and I managed to stay quite a distance from my dad. When I did see him, for example at breakfast or tea, he would ask, 'You behaving, Tracy? Hope you're not annoying anyone?'

I liked the fresh air and the smell of the woods; even the cooking smelled good after a day of excursions. The adults would have a few beers but this was after the kids were asleep. I only knew about it because some of the older boys would pinch cans when their backs were turned and then brag about it next day.

Dad never called me a 'good girl' or asked me to be a good girl on the trip, maybe because he knew he couldn't get to me without someone noticing. This alleviated some of the anxiety I felt but I still kept my guard up; what if it was all a ploy? What if he was only keeping away from me so that I did take my eye off the ball and someone else got to me? It never happened. No one touched me, no one did anything inappropriate – even Dad was just as he should have always been, but I think the awful thing about that trip was the terrible fear I had in advance. I was so sure, so convinced that nothing normal could happen in my life that I had made myself believe that I was walking into a paedophile ring. How awful is that? How twisted is it that a child should be certain such things exist everywhere? When other mums got ill, I truly thought that was because their daughters weren't being 'good girls' with their own fathers. When another mum was taken away to hospital, I looked for signs to prove that the blame could be laid at the door of the child. I saw these signs, even where there were none, and as my own mother continued to be ill, and continued to feel nothing but dislike for me, it gave me even more 'proof'.

I was on tenterhooks that whole weekend, but I must be totally honest and say that I also enjoyed a great deal of it. When I felt that I was in a group, when I stuck by Deborah, or made sure there were other children nearby at all times, I could let myself be a kid again. I did start to feel safer because, looking around and scoping things out, I began to feel that Dad simply wouldn't be able to beckon me away if he felt like it. Someone would notice and that made me feel more secure. It didn't help with my anxiety though; I always had a knot in my stomach.

There were two girls on the trip who were orphans. I was drawn to them in particular, because they represented my worst nightmare. Their mums had done exactly what I worried about more than anything – they had died. One night, when we were in our sleeping bags, I started up a conversation with the girls, which finally led to the point I'd been heading for all along.

'Were your mums really ill before they died?' I asked. 'Were they in hospital a lot, and did it get worse?'

'No,' said the younger of the two. 'My mammy got run over one day by a hit-and-run driver. She was never ill.'

'Was she not ill before the accident?' I asked.

'No – she was fine. Why?'

'I just wondered,' I told her. 'What about you? Was your mum ill a lot?' I enquired of the other girl.

'She was pregnant – that seemed to last a while,' she told me. 'Then she went into hospital to have my little brother and she never came home. She died having him.'

'Had you been bad?' I wondered aloud.

'Bad?' she repeated.

'Well . . . before your mum died,' I went on, with a complete lack of tact, 'did your dad say that something bad would happen if you kept being bad?'

She looked completely confused by what I was saying.

'I never really see my dad – he's always at work. My granny looks after me and my brother most of the time; even when Mum was around, Granny was there. Mum died because of the baby, there was some sort of problem – how could she have died because I was bad, and how would my dad know?'

How could I explain any of this to them? I had genuinely believed so much of what Dad had told me. The only way I could explain *dead* mummies was through the bad behaviour of their daughters – I didn't know anything else. Mums who died in childbirth or through car crashes were much stranger to me than the notion of mums who could die because daughters didn't allow their fathers to abuse them.

The camping trip had to end, and I had to go back to reality. I hadn't seen much of Gary while we were away, but Mum's reaction to his return would have made anyone think he'd been on a year-long expedition, while I may have just as well have popped to the corner shop. She was all over him, showering her boy with hugs and kisses, telling him how much she'd missed him and telling him of all the treats waiting for him.

She looked at me as if she had something dirty on her shoe. With a sigh, she said, 'Oh, well, I suppose it's back to running after you all day long. Nice while it lasted. You'll be as needy as ever,' she moaned. I guess she was torn. To get rid of me, she'd had to put up with Gary's absence too and that was something she found very hard indeed. The relief that I hadn't been abused on the trip was something I could hold on to, but the different look on Mum's face when she saw me as opposed to Gary was horrible. As I stood there, without so much as a kindly word of welcome back, I wondered if she had any idea of the depth of my love for her? I had done such things, allowed such things to be done to me, all for the love of this woman who could barely bring herself to be in the same room as me. I would have moved mountains for her. If she had spent one day treating me the way she treated Gary *every* day, then I

76

would have been able to bear things knowing that she loved me. They wouldn't have been easier – how could they have been? – but it cut me to the quick that she still seemed to hate me when I was trying so hard to keep her well and out of hospital. Didn't she know that, without me, she would be parted from Gary even more? I kept quiet about my sexual abuse, thinking that I was saving a mother who never gave me the time of day.

The trip came with repercussions, as did most things. When we got home, we were both excited. Gary couldn't wait to tell Mum all that had gone on.

'It was brilliant!' he said. 'There was canoeing, archery, pony trekking, and loads more, Mum!'

'It was really good—' I tried to join in.

'Shut up, Tracy, let Gary talk without interruption,' snapped Mum.

'But I went orienteering and pony trekking too, Mum, I made friends and—'

'Shut up, Tracy!' she yelled.

Mum wouldn't listen to a word I had to say while Gary was there, but Dad picked up on the last part about me and the girls, and I watched his face as the anger spread over it. He said nothing at that point and I hoped it had passed.

However, a few days later, the storm hit.

'Those girls were *not* friends of yours, Tracy, and you will *not* be seeing them again. That whole trip was an exercise that the Army had come up with to keep good relations, not to indulge silly little girls like you – do you hear me? I'm telling you now – forget these troublemakers and anyone else you met, because I can promise you that you will never see them again. I'll make sure of that.'

I was terrified of him, and could have kicked myself for letting slip that I had made any friends in the first place.

'Did you behave?' he asked me, and I nodded quickly to show that I had been good.

He had been there the whole time but I guess that, when I raised the point about making friends, he wondered what had been going on when he couldn't keep a close eye on me. 'You sure you didn't say anything untoward? You didn't tell our secret?' He answered himself almost immediately. 'No, you wouldn't want Mum to get ill again, would you?'

'No, no, I wouldn't, I wouldn't do anything to make her sick, Dad.'

'Good – now get over here.'

He was unzipping his trousers as I walked towards him, and I knew what he wanted – I knew what he always wanted. He grabbed my hand and placed it on him. He moved my hand up and down, up and down, as he chanted, 'Keep the secret, keep the secret.' When it was finally over, I rushed to the bathroom and washed my hands, rubbing the soap over and over, desperately trying to rid myself of the smell and the stickiness, even if the memories couldn't be so easily removed.

Soon everything was back to how it always was. I wonder whether Dad ever thought it would all blow up in his face? He must surely have thought that, at some point, I would realise Mum didn't care about me and then question why I was doing this for her. The very idea that I was willing to trade my abuse for her health was appalling – but what was just as appalling was that she never saw the broken little girl in front of her, desperate for any crumb of affection she could get.

CHAPTER 5

ALL DOLLED UP

There were certain realities of Army life that affected how I was living – if you haven't any familiarity with that sort of environment it may seem strange, but there were aspects of that world which, I believe, made it easier for abuse to happen. The first thing which helped it all to remain secret was that the men – and they were mostly men at that time, the women tended to just work as secretaries and suchlike – who were full-timers had an aura of 'hero' about them. No matter what they did, they all got treated as good men, brave and strong, even the ones like my dad who did nothing but sit in an office all day. I'm not denying for a moment that there were heroes, there were good, brave, strong soldiers, but Dad wasn't one of them. This atmosphere made it even less likely that anyone would ever believe me. I was just a child and, on top of that, a child who was gaining a reputation as being smelly, disruptive, and difficult. If anyone had to choose whether to believe a child like that or my father, I would lose.

The second aspect of Army life that made it harder for my abuse to be seen was that families kept themselves to themselves. Friendships were made quickly and left behind quickly – you couldn't get too attached to anyone, because you never knew when you would be posted somewhere else. You had to be able to pick up friends easily, and for that reason no one liked to rock the boat. The women went to their bingo nights, they sold Avon to each other and they traded recipes – they may have muttered complaints about their husbands under their breaths, or after a few sherries, but that was a world away from a child standing up and saying that her father was a paedophile. There was a terror of anyone being seen as different. The group mentality which pervaded that environment allowed abuse of all kinds to flourish – plenty of women hid black eyes, and plenty of neighbours turned a deaf ear to the sounds of violence through the walls.

On top of that, the life was very insular. Even if you lived in Germany, Northern Ireland, Singapore or else-where, you were an Army kid on a British base. You went to a school with other children in the same position and you stuck with them. You rarely learned the local language, and you maintained a strong feeling of superiority over the locals. If something happened outside the base, you would be returned to the confines and rules of your own little world. Even the houses were the same on every base. After a night out drinking once, Dad actually went into someone else's flat, thinking it was ours, and fell asleep, drunk, in their front room. There was so little individuality that no one really thought anything of it!

All of these things combined to make a small world in which I felt completely insignificant and alone; Dad was doing all he could to keep it that way. During the time we spent in Northern Ireland, his abuse of me seemed to be developing. It was as if he was thinking of new things to do, new ways to touch or terrorise me. When Mum was at bingo, and Gary was at his youth club, I generally assumed that something would happen. And I was usually right.

'Get to your bed!' he shouted one night.

He always shouted at me these days, unless he was doing something to me. At those times, he would sometimes try to use a gentler voice, but it wouldn't matter to me; I knew what was underneath it, and I knew what a monster he had become.

It was early, Mum and Gary had just left, but I knew better than to challenge him. If he said it was bedtime, it was bedtime. I could only hope that I was indeed going to be left alone to sleep, but I doubted it; if he was sending me away so early, long before Mum and Gary got back, I feared the worst.

Silently, I went to my room. I quickly got into my pyjamas, buttoned them up to the top, then run as fast as I could to the loo where I also brushed my teeth in record time. I whizzed back to my bed, leaping in and drawing the covers up close to my chin.

I could hear his footsteps coming along the hall.

I could hear him a mile away.

I closed my eyes and made an attempt at looking as if I was fast asleep, while the door creaked open. I knew he was standing there long before he said anything.

'Close your curtains, Tracy,' he told me.

I'd left them open in the hope that he might think someone could see in. It was a pathetic attempt to control the situation and it could be overcome in seconds, but I still always hoped that I would find a little thing that would change the outcome.

I got out of bed and did as he asked, then scuttled back across the floor to wrap myself in the bedclothes again.

The silence went on.

After another minute or so, he said, 'Get out of bed and stand in the middle of the room.'

There was no point feigning sleep – I'd risk a battering if I did that, and I would have to keep quiet for that too.

Again, I did as I was told.

'Take your pyjamas off,' he said. His voice was cold and controlled. He didn't sound as if he wasn't aware of what he was doing; he sounded as if he had it all planned out in advance. I did sometimes wonder if he thought all of the scenarios through before he carried out his abuses.

I stood there shivering. I think I would've shivered no matter what time of year it was, because the shivering was coming from inside me, from the fear of not knowing what he had planned for me. I have heard other abuse survivors say that one of the horrors for them is that moment when they actually wish the attack would happen – not because they want it in any way, but because the waiting and the knowledge that what is about to take place is absolutely guaranteed is heartbreaking. That is exactly how I felt that night.

Bizarrely, he did nothing.

He didn't make me touch him and he didn't touch me.

After I'd taken off my pyjamas, he made sure the door was closed, walked fully into the room, and switched on my bedside lamp. I felt so ashamed that he could see me. He sat on the bed he had just ordered me out of, and stared at me in complete silence. Some more time passed (one minute, five minutes, ten minutes – it all felt like a lifetime), then he spoke again.

'Turn around, Tracy.'

I did. I turned around fully, in a circle.

'Now, turn around and look at me.'

I did that too.

'Turn around so that your back is to me.'

I followed that instruction.

'Now, stand absolutely still, facing the wall.'

He gave me all of these orders a few times. He said nothing other than those commands, with his hands in his lap. Finally, he told me to get dressed and get into bed.

He walked back to the door as I put my pyjamas on and climbed under the covers, then he left the room.

About a week later, he did the same thing. Once it was over that time, he spoke.

'You like me looking at you.' It was a statement, not a question. 'I know that you like it when you undress for me.'

I was so scared as well as very cold when this went on, and I felt such humiliation. I may not have known the word back then, but I know it now – and I suspect that was exactly what he wanted me to feel. During this 'procedure', I would often be visibly shivering, yet this never deterred him. I was thinking to myself, why is he doing this? What does he want? Is he going to hurt me? I never questioned him out loud though as I knew better by now and it would only have resulted in getting slapped.

One day I got home from school and no one was in the living room. I sat down at the table and got my homework out of my school bag, hoping to get a bit of peace before things kicked off. It seemed like there was always something stopping me from concentrating on schoolwork – Dad 'at' me, Mum shouting at me, Gary tormenting me – but, on this occasion, I remembered that Mum had said she was going into town for some things and wouldn't be there when I got back. It was Gary's afternoon for football practice at school, and I could only pray that Dad was still at work. There had been no sound from him when I got in, and I couldn't see any opened tins of beer or smell any fresh smoke in the room.

I had just organised my books and pencils, and settled a bit, when I heard a creaking from the bedroom. His bedroom. I paused and held my breath. Maybe he was having a nap. Maybe he was just moving in his sleep.

No chance.

Just as I breathed out again, he called for me.

'Tracy! Tracy, come here!' he yelled.

'I'm busy, Dad,' I replied. 'I've got homework to do.'

'Get through here! I'll tell you when you're busy and when you're not,' he answered, using his usual logic.

When I walked in, he was lying on the bed that he shared with Mum. *At least he's dressed*, I thought to myself.

'Come here,' he snapped.

'I'll get changed first,' I said. I was still in my school uniform and trying to find an excuse to leave the room.

'Don't bother,' he replied. 'I said, come here.'

'But Mum—' I began.

'She's in town, shopping, as you probably bloody know, and Gary's at football practice, as you probably already bloody know as well. Stop gabbing, and get over here.'

I walked slowly towards him. I could only hope it was quick – and surely it would be, as Mum wouldn't be out for too long?

'I want you to put some lipstick on,' he told me as I sat down on the side of the bed.

'I don't have any lipstick,' I countered, 'and I wouldn't be allowed to wear it if I had.'

'Valerie has some,' he told me. I noticed that he said 'Valerie' instead of 'your mum'. It was as if he was trying to distance the relationship, given whatever he was no doubt planning to do.

'I can't use Mum's lipstick!' I said, shocked. 'She'd kill me!'

'Don't bother about *Valerie*,' he emphasised, 'do as I tell you.'

I knew that Mum actually only had one lipstick that she kept for special occasions, not that there were many of those. I also knew that she kept it in her vanity case in her wardrobe. I had sneaked a look at it before. It was pink and, naturally, from Avon. Dad told me to get it – telling me where it was, even though I already knew – and I hesitantly opened the vanity case and removed it.

'Open it,' he told me.

'Dad . . .' I began.

'Do as I FUCKING say!' he shouted.

I opened the little cardboard box carefully, terrified that I might rip it and Mum would know. There was always this two-sided feeling to everything. I didn't want her to know as I would get into trouble – but, surely, if she did know, she would question what was going on, and maybe all would come out into the open?

The lipstick had a strong, sweet smell. This should've been fun for a little girl, trying out her mum's make-up. It should have been Mum there, not Dad, and it should all have felt very, very different. Mum never let me near the little make-up she did possess, but I still had that yearning that one day she would, that one day we would do lovely things together. I knew that whatever Dad had planned would be a world away from lovely.

He told me to take the lipstick and sit at the dressing table so I could see myself putting it on.

I sat down and he said, 'You look like your mother, sitting there.' My back was to him but he could see me in the mirror and I could see him. He was staring at me without blinking.

I sat and carefully put the lipstick on, puckering my lips as I had seen the ladies do on TV, taking care not to smudge it, on my lips or on the actual lipstick itself, as Mum might have suspected something. In any other circumstances I would have been delighted to do this and play at being a grown-up or a mummy, but I didn't know exactly what lay ahead. What did he want? What would I have to do? The apprehension was building and I could feel my stomach churning.

'Now turn around,' he said, once I had applied it.

I did.

'You look pretty,' Dad said. 'So pretty. You look older. Still a little whore though, aren't you?'

As he started his usual litany of insults against me (and, for me, telling me that I was his good girl was now an insult too), I could see that he had his trousers undone and was masturbating himself.

'Come here and give me a kiss with your luscious lips,' he leered. He often used words like that, words which sounded odd coming from him. I wondered whether he had got them from magazines or from television. 'Here, sit down beside me.'

As I walked across to him, he said, 'You're my beautiful woman, you look great, my own beautiful woman, that's what you are.'

I sat down and he grabbed my head from behind and brought my face down to his. He kissed me, gently at first then harder. I tried to pull away as I couldn't breathe properly but he held me there until he was finished, then he started masturbating himself again as he looked at me. I was relieved that he wasn't touching me or making me touch him, but it was still disgusting to hear his noises, to listen to those foul words come out of his mouth, and to know that he was doing that because of what he was thinking about me. This, this was my first kiss really, and it was with my own father – and he seemed to see nothing wrong in it.

'You're such a pretty lady, aren't you? You look nice, so nice, but listen – you only ever put lipstick on for me, OK?' he said, once he had finished.

'Yes, Dad,' I said quietly, 'can I go now?'

'Aye, you can – but put the lipstick back where you got it before you bugger off.'

He pushed me off the bed so hard that I fell on to his boots that were lying on the floor, hurting my backside. Crying and ashamed, I put the lipstick back exactly as I had found it. By the time I had put it away, Dad had left the room and was in the bathroom. I went into my room and got changed, then into the living room. I had made one mistake – I had forgotten to take the lipstick off. When he walked into the room and saw me, Dad came lunging at me, slapped me hard, knocking me sideways.

'You stupid fucking bitch! Get that shit off your lips before your mother comes back. Now!' he yelled.

I was so confused and hurt, not just from the slap that left my face stinging, but at how he could change so quickly. Ten minutes earlier, things had been so different and I just could never comprehend these swift changes in him. If he really wanted me to believe he loved me and that he was a good father, why didn't he keep that angle going for longer? Why did it have to end with him hitting me so often?

Mum didn't find out about the lipstick or, if she did suspect, she never said anything. Her obsession with getting out of the house was increasing at this time. If she wasn't at a Tupperware party, she was at bingo. If she wasn't at bingo, she was at an Avon party. If she wasn't at an Avon party, she was off to a Pippa Dee night at someone's house.

Pippa Dee was the original party-plan event. One of the women would invite everyone to her house, lay out little dishes of nibbles and drinks, and hope that they would all buy lots of things. There were leaflets showing the 'best' items and a rep from the company would have a case of clothes to show off. Everything seemed to be made of nylon and it was all in bright, 1970s colours. I think anything white and cotton would have been banned – lime green polyester was the order of the day!

The hostess received a percentage of the sales. I think she could either take this in cash, or buy Pippa Dee items of greater value with it. Someone at the party would be persuaded into booking a party at theirs, and the same thing would happen the next week or the next month. Round and round it went, with most people hosting and everyone buying things for the sake of it. The Pippa Dee rep would always say that no one was under any obligation, but it was as if buying something vile and scratchy was the entrance fee for a night out, so each woman would join in.

Mum didn't host these parties – she would never have been allowed to have a group of women round at our house, drinking and laughing, having a good time and enjoying themselves – but she did go to a lot of them, just as she went to any other party being held by any other woman. It was all part of forming those friendships.

In Northern Ireland especially, the women needed each other. They never knew if their men would be coming home. They never knew when they would turn on the television or radio and hear of a bomb which would rip their family apart. They couldn't wander around, being open about where they lived and what their husbands did. They were prisoners in a lot of ways, and they could trust no one apart from the other Army wives. When someone new came into the group, they were welcomed with open arms, because no one knew what was coming next. You never knew when you might need that person to help you out, look after your kids while you rushed to hospital to see if your man had made it, or keep them for a few days while you made funeral arrangements.

Of course, my dad wasn't really one of these men. No matter what you think of the politics of 1970s Northern Ireland, there is no denying that a lot of people lost loved ones. Every soldier was a father or a son or a husband or a friend, and they all had someone who cared for them, but Dad wasn't a brave soldier. He was sitting in an office, in no real danger, day in and day out. You could argue that the barracks might have been bombed, or that he was in danger of being attacked when he left the compound, but that applied to all of us. His life was in no more jeopardy than mine.

One night, while Mum was out, I was lying in bed. Listening. I was always listening. I listened for him moving. I listened for the floorboards creaking. I listened for his footsteps coming along the hall to my bedroom. This is a terrible thing for an abused child. Not knowing what will happen, not knowing if *it* will happen that day or that night brings terror. That night, I heard him. He was in the living room, drinking and smoking as usual, and had barely grunted when Mum left. I have no idea where my brother was. Gary had so much more freedom than I did, and he tended to just run in for food then rush out again without even having to say where he was going. I listened as Dad threw an empty beer can. It probably didn't hit the empties box. He didn't really care, as there was always someone to clean up after him. I heard the television being turned off – or, at least, I heard the absence of the noise from it after a few seconds. Then I heard him.

There was nowhere to go, nowhere to run. I just had to wait really. Wait for it to be over then wait for it to happen again. I tucked my pyjama top into my pyjama bottoms, a futile gesture, but an attempt at keeping myself covered up, then burrowed into the bedclothes. The room was dark – I always tried to avoid drawing attention to myself – and I shook as he clicked the switch on.

'Tracy! What the fuck are you doing in here in the dark?' he snarled.

I breathed heavily and tried to make some snoring noises in a lame attempt to make him think I was asleep. It wouldn't have mattered if I was; he would never just give up and go away.

'Get up!' he shouted, pulling the covers off me.

'I'm asleep, Dad, I'm asleep,' I whimpered.

'You're a fucking liar, that's what you are,' he replied. 'Get through to my room – go on, move it!'

I tried to pull the covers up onto me again but he dragged it back, slapping my leg as he did so, and telling me once more to go to his bedroom. I did hesitate. Even though I knew I could never stop him from doing what he wanted, it still went against everything in me to willingly, happily and easily walk to my fate. He clenched his fingers on my upper arm and, as I squealed in pain, he yanked me off the mattress and pulled me behind him.

Every part of me was screaming against it – my body was rigid, I was crying, I was shouting 'No, Dad, no!' As usual, it made no difference. 'Come on then, that's a good girl,' he said as we slowly made our way along the hallway, him pulling me as I resisted as much as I could. There is absolutely no way he could have thought I was initiating this. 'You're a wee devil, aren't you? A right wee fucking tease, you are. Christ, I barely get a minute's peace with you.'

He threw me on the bed in the room he shared with Mum.

'Ah, go on then, let's get you sorted. Christ, you're wearing me out, aren't you? Fucking well can't get enough, can you?'

He sat on the edge of the bed too as I scurried as far away from him as possible. I didn't know what he was up to. He continued to talk to me as if I was an adult woman, not a child. He told me that I couldn't get enough, that I exhausted him with my demands. It was as if he was trying to turn me into what he wanted from a woman, while in complete denial that I was a terrified child. His eyes narrowed as if he was thinking about something – I suspected I knew what it was. Since he had started to try and make me act like a willing, adult partner in his disgusting sex sessions, it was as if he was thinking things through each time. I had hated the way he had made me kiss him the previous week when he acted as if we were a couple, not a twisted father hurting his daughter. I didn't want to make out as if he was someone I loved, some romantic hero who had swept me off my feet. I hated the tongues, the words, the touching, but I felt that was exactly what he was gearing up to do again.

'Here, I know what we'll do,' he said, 'you'll like this. You're a woman now, aren't you, Tracy? And women like nice things, they do, they like nice things . . .'

He got off the bed and wandered over to the wardrobe in the corner. He rummaged about in it for a little while, then took out a brightly coloured bag with 'Pippa Dee' written on the side.

'Your mum's,' he said, shaking another plastic bag out of the first one. It landed on the bed and he smiled. 'Christ, you women! You love your frilly things, dressing up, making filthy tarts of yourselves . . .'

With that, he ripped the plastic open and out spilled a bright pink, frothy negligee. It was what we called a 'baby-doll' back then. I had never witnessed my mum in such a thing, but I had seen women in magazines and catalogues, as well as on TV, wearing them. They were terribly glamorous and very feminine. They were low-cut and short, they kicked out at the thigh and, no doubt for many couples, were a symbol of happy, normal, fun bedroom activity between consenting adults.

'Put it on,' he said, throwing it at me.

I shook my head.

'It's Mum's,' I whispered.

'You're the woman of the house when she's not here. Put it on, and pull it up.'

I shook my head again.

'She'll go mad,' I said.

'Is that what you're worried about?' he snorted. 'Leave her to me. Put it on. Now.' As I hesitated, he leaned towards me. 'I'm not joking, Tracy. If you want to keep the use of your fucking legs, get that on.'

I did. The labels were still attached and they scratched me as I pulled the negligee over my head. It was massive on me – I was only nine, and not particularly tall for my age – and it looked like a fancy-dress costume.

'Look at you,' he leered. 'You little fucking slut. Desperate for it, aren't you? Dressing up like a whore – that's what you need to be treated like then, isn't it?'

It seemed as if he went on in this vein forever. Telling me what he would do to me, how I wanted it, how he was just doing what I was after, how it was all my fault. All the time, he touched me. His hands were all over me, his fingers hurting me as he pushed and prodded.

My mum's special negligee was pushed up and I couldn't help thinking, *She'll kill me if this gets ripped.*

'You look fucking gorgeous like that,' he said, 'all dolled up for me.' He reached down to unbuckle his belt and take his trousers off. I couldn't stand it. It wasn't really that he was doing anything new, but the fact that I was in their bed, dressed as Mum, while he told me that I was the woman of the house with all that entailed, just seemed too much.

As he fumbled with his pants, I jumped off the bed and ran towards the door.

'Where the fuck do you think you're going?' he shouted as I kept running. I got to my own room and pulled the negligee over my head.

'I don't want this! I don't want you to do this to me!' I wept, over and over.

'Tough fucking luck,' he hissed. 'Now get your tart's nightie back on and shut the fuck up. Christ, the bother you cause me, Tracy . . .'

As he spoke, I heard a key in the door. Mum! I shoved the babydoll into my own wardrobe as he pulled his trousers up from where they had been hanging round one ankle as he'd chased me.

'Harry?' came a voice from the hallway. 'That's me back – where are you?'

'In here, Valerie!' he called to her. 'In wee Tracy's room!'

I couldn't believe he was telling her where we were. What would I do with the negligee, what if she found it?

'Is she playing up again, Harry?' asked Mum as she appeared at my door. 'What's she up to now? God, that child will be the death of me.'

'Don't you worry about it, Val,' he replied. 'Leave her to me. You just sit down and have a cup of tea. I'll deal with this wee bastard.'

'What's she done?' asked Mum, coming into the room and peering at me.

'I'm trying to get to the bottom of it,' he said. 'I heard her rummaging around in our room and when I went through, she scooted out. She had something in her hand, but I don't know what, she won't tell me.'

'Did she now? The wee bitch!' shouted Mum, rushing back to her own bedroom. 'If she's touched any of my things . . . Has she been at my Avon?'

I heard her voice trail off as Dad smiled at me.

'Tut-tut, Tracy,' he whispered. 'You're in trouble now, aren't you? What a shame, what a shame.'

'Harry! Harry!' Mum shrieked. 'Look what's she done!' She came back into my room holding the ripped plastic bags. 'She's been in my wardrobe! She's found my Pippa Dee! She's taken my . . . my . . . well, my new special nightie!'

Looking shocked, Dad opened my wardrobe as I sat on the floor, aghast at what was playing out in front of me.

'Would you look at that, Valerie?' he said, pulling the negligee out. 'That's shocking behaviour, it really is.'

Mum shook her head and looked ready to explode.

'I'm at the end of my tether with her, I really am. Why does she do this to me? Why does she torment me? I'm not a well woman, Harry – I can't take this.'

'I know, Val, I know,' he soothed. 'You see, I think she just wants to be like her mummy. Dressing up, pretending to be you, it's just what wee lassies do. No harm really, nothing's damaged.'

I never said a word. There was no point.

He put his hand on her back and guided her out of the door.

'You go and have that cup of tea,' he said. 'Calm your nerves. Leave Tracy to me. I'll sort her. I'll give her what she deserves. Off you go.'

I closed my eyes, and awaited my fate once more.

Mum was closing her eyes to all of it too. Dad continued with this new slant on his abuse of me – he continued to insist that I wanted it, that I was encouraging him, that I was a woman who needed satisfying. As I got older, I questioned more – mostly to myself, but I did sometimes ask him why Mum was ill when I was doing everything he asked.

'I'm not a fucking doctor,' he'd reply. 'Just watch yourself.'

That meant the same things as always – don't tell, do what he wanted, pretend to enjoy it. He hated it when I showed any sign of having a life away from him. I had started chatting to a girl called Hilary who lived opposite us, and that was something he couldn't bear. One day, when he saw me talking outside with Hilary, he knocked on the window and beckoned for me to come inside.

'You seem very cosy,' he said. 'You do remember what I've said, Tracy? You can't tell anyone about helping your mum. If you do, she'll get ill again. She could die – and it would be your fault. Just remember that next time you're gossiping with your little friend.'

I said I would remember and casually turned to go back to Hilary.

'Where the hell are you pissing off to now, you stupid little bitch?' he snapped. 'Get to my room. Your mum's not been feeling too well at all – move it.'

He started muttering *filthy, whore, bitch, slut* as usual and I, like the good little girl I was, made to lie down on the bed when we got to his room. He told me to sit up, took off his trousers and pants, and positioned himself in a sitting stance too, up by the headboard. I tried not to look at what was between his legs and blurted out that I didn't want to touch him.

'Is that right?' he smiled. 'Well, it's fine – but it is about time you used your mouth for something other than complaining.' With that, he grabbed me by the hair and pulled me towards his penis.

'No!' I shouted when it dawned on me what he wanted to do. I actually only thought he wanted me to kiss it, and that was bad enough, but when he started to call me a whore and told me to open my mouth, the full horror of it struck me. I could hardly move my head so I thrashed my body around, trying to avoid him, avoid *that*, but he was strong.

'Listen, your mother will fucking die if you don't do this. Get your fucking mouth open and get it round that – you'll know what to do once you start.'

He kept my head at his penis but I just couldn't do it. I gave it a quick little kiss then started to sob. He said I was enjoying it, that I was a dirty slut who loved it, but when he forced it into my mouth, I gagged. I could feel vomit rising in my throat and there was a light-headedness over-whelming me. He finally threw me off him.

'For fuck's sake! That's supposed to be nice for me and you've fucking ruined it.'

With that, he pulled his clothes up and stormed out of the room.

Nice? For him?

Wasn't it to make Mum better?

Something dawned on me in that moment. If this was about him, if this was about things being *nice* for *him*, then Mum wouldn't get better, no matter what I did.

CHAPTER 6

NORMAL LIFE

Dad hit me a lot in Northern Ireland – in fact, I still have a rib out of place from the batterings I took. He wasn't just sexually abusing me, he was mentally torturing me, physically harming me, verbally lambasting me. He would do anything he could to keep me in check, but the comment he had made about it being 'nice' had set me thinking. Was this all really for Mum? She wasn't so ill in Northern Ireland and had spent a lot of time out of the house. Dad encouraged this as it gave him free rein with me, but he could see that things were changing. Slowly, but surely, I was less willing to do as I was told. I smiled less, I pretended less. I never let him force me into oral sex and I believe that the fact it had gone wrong on the first occasion protected me to some extent from it happening again.

Naively, I failed to realise that there were more things he could do – and that he would always win. If Mum left for bingo early, I would always try to avoid being with him, so I would go to my room and read, or pretend to be asleep, no matter how early it was. Of course, this didn't always work, and he would do what he wanted to anyway, but on one occasion I foolishly pushed things too far.

'I'll just read for five minutes and then put my light out,' I said to Dad as I went to my room. I regretted my words as soon as they were out of my mouth.

'Will you now?' he replied. 'And when did you get to call the shots? Disobeying me again. Why are you such a bad girl, Tracy? *I'll* tell you when to put the light off.'

I cursed myself as I walked away, wishing I'd said nothing. When he appeared in my room later that night, when he climbed on top of me, I knew I'd pay the price – I just had no idea how high that price would be. I sensed something that night. There was a change in his mood, his attitude, his presence, which panicked me and I tried to push him off my body. He said nothing, just forced himself on top of me a little more strongly before starting to touch me all over. He pushed my nightdress up and his horrible nicotine-stained fingers found their way inside my pants. He pulled those off and started hurting me so badly; he was rougher than I could ever remember. His fingers were going so much further than ever before; I didn't think I could stand it. Dad was panting and getting out of breath, while I just prayed it would all be over soon.

He took off everything we were both wearing. I was so worried I could barely breathe. I'd hoped the rough touching would have made him finish much more quickly, but it now looked as if he planned to be here for a while. He lay on his side and I lay on my back, staring at the ceiling. The stink of him was awful.

As I lay there, he stroked my hair and called me his little whore. I told him I didn't want to do this, I was explicit telling him that, but he kept saying that Mum would get ill and it would be my fault. She had been saying she felt unwell that week, and I was torn: I was beginning to feel that this was all about what Dad wanted, not Mum's illness, but I was also terrified that if I challenged it at all, she would die.

He kept up his chant of sexual insults and said I loved all of this, then began to shove his fingers inside me again. It was intrusive and hideous. I started gagging again just at the thought of what might be about to happen, even though I didn't know exactly what it would be. He ignored me and climbed on top. 'You're Daddy's girl,' he said, 'you're my little darling.' I could feel that he was hard and I could feel that he was pushing his penis into me – then he entered me. I thought the pain was going to split me into little pieces. I didn't think I could survive it. All the time he was thrusting, he was saying that I was a whore, a bitch, his whore, his bitch. I was nine years old.

It seemed to take forever for him to finish. When he finally got off me, I think I was in shock. Not just with pain, but with the realisation that this was what he would now want to do. He never went backwards, he only ever upped his game.

Dad – my dad, the father who had just raped me – left the room, only to return with a washing basin filled with hot water, a flannel and some soap. He washed between my legs, constantly muttering *little prostitute, little prostitute.*

'You'll see,' he said to me, 'Mum will be fine now.'

I didn't believe him any more. I didn't believe any of it.

Mum came back. Gary came back. Dad sat in the living room, smoking and drinking. I listened to it all going on and wept until I could weep no more.

Life went on – it always did. There was violence in my home life and there was violence on the streets of Northern Ireland. Unrest was everywhere, and tensions ran high until eventually they boiled over on 30 January 1972. Bloody Sunday changed life for so many people. For us, it meant a move back to Rinteln, announced by Mum the day after the killings.

'Right, get packing,' she announced. 'We've got a week to get out of this hellhole.'

And get out we did. Our new home was on a different base, still in Rinteln, but it looked the same as they all did. Things weren't getting any better, but I was getting older and that, in itself, brought changes. Dad's luck held and Mum stayed out of hospital for about six months after he first raped me, which was extremely confusing. Just as I'd started to question whether there was a link, it seemed as if there was. His constant abuse of me wasn't without repercussions – mentally and emotionally, I was in pieces, even if I did keep it to myself, and physically I was often covered in bruises. Something had to give – my body needed someone to pay attention to what was happening. One morning, quite soon after we returned to Rinteln, I woke up feeling awful; there was nothing specific, just a feeling that something wasn't right. I was aching all over and had terrible stomach cramps, I was having breathing problems and panic attacks.

Mum called the doctor and, when he arrived, she and Dad stood just inside the bedroom door throughout the visit. He didn't give me much of an examination and announced it was a tummy bug. Dad chatted the whole time, trying to distract him I guess, and I was never left alone with the doctor. If I had been, would he have looked a bit harder? Would he have seen the bruises under my nightdress? Would he have seen any of the enormous damage that had been inflicted on my body?

As the doctor got up to leave, I made one attempt at making him see there was something terribly wrong.

'I'm smelly, I smell, I smell all over, I smell,' I groaned.

It was as if I could see the colour drain from my dad's face. Mum interrupted, 'What's she saying, Harry, what's she saying?'

I tried again.

'I smell so bad.'

'What do you mean?' the doctor asked.

Dad walked quickly over to my bed, grasped my hand and dug his nails into it as he squeezed it. 'Valerie puts all her Avon stuff in here – pomanders and soaps and things. Terrible stink, I'll get it all cleared out.'

The doctor accepted it without question and left. Dad swept up all of the smelly things and took away the one bit of Mum that I kept with me in my room.

That was a wake-up call for me. I was getting nowhere being a good girl. Dad ignored me when I said no, and he pinned me down when I struggled. The only way I could think to disobey him was by making friends at school. There were two girls I latched on to quite quickly once I'd made my decision. Holly Barton was a captain's daughter from a really well-respected family. She was always friendly towards me and we started to hang out together. Holly was a little bit wayward and I liked her because of this – we played chap door run, we broke windows on abandoned buildings and stole sweets. Little things to her, but big things to me at that stage. Holly and another girl called Glenda Miller would show me that you could have a good time being naughty. They encouraged me to shoplift and I managed to get a huge amount of make-up and chocolate one weekend when we went into town. Unsurprisingly, Mum caught me hiding the spoils.

'What's this? Have you been stealing?' she asked.

'It's nothing, nothing – I've done nothing wrong,' I protested.

'Well, that's fine then, you won't be bothered about me calling the police.'

And that was exactly what she did. I denied it all but then Dad came in – he asked if he could have a quick word with me. I admitted everything to him – I was more scared of my father than the police – and he told them he would deal with it, which they accepted.

It was as if he could persuade anyone to believe him. Even the police acted as if he was a man to be respected. I was scared for a while after the shoplifting incident and I was well punished in the ways he preferred, but when I was with Holly and Glenda, they made it all seem a laugh. I never told them of the abuse, but they just made me feel normal.

I decided to do even more naughty things, so I began causing more damage in abandoned buildings, as well as breaking windows and fixtures in new-build houses on an empty estate, and setting fires there. I was just trying to find a way to make my voice heard without actually saying the words that I was sure no one would want to hear.

I remember one time, when I was eleven – nearly twelve – my mother had bought me a pair of new flared trousers from the NAAFI. It was rare for her to buy me anything but there was a school disco coming up – the combination of me constantly asking for some flares and her being keen to present a good image of our family worked, and I was delighted when the flowing trousers were finally bought. I couldn't remember the last time I'd had something new. In fact, I was well known for being almost exclusively dressed in Gary's hand-me-downs, to the extent that a horrible boy on the school bus, Patrick, started calling me second-hand Rose, and encouraged all the others to do so, while mocking what I wore. These trousers could change all of that, I felt.

I paraded around in my room with them on, admiring myself in the mirror and hugging myself with delight. I couldn't help myself from wearing them more and more at home, rather than keep them pristine for the disco, and so started wearing them all around the house. One day, when I got home from school, Dad was sprawled in his chair when I opened the door.

'Your mum's back in hospital,' he said, sharply.

I muttered something vague and went into my room, closing the door behind me. I pulled on my new trousers and did my usual twirl in front of the mirror, delighted with myself. I could hear the noise of the television coming from the living room, so assumed that Dad was busy; I got out my homework and finished that, still in my new trousers, and then heard him call, 'Tracy! Get the dinner on!'

As I went to change into my scruffy, at-home clothes, I had a thought. I could wear my new trousers for as long as I liked, as Mum wasn't here to catch me and say that I needed to keep them for the disco. Within minutes, I regretted my decision. Making chips for everyone, some hot fat splattered onto my trousers and, no matter, how much I rubbed at them, the stain wouldn't come off – in fact, I was making it worse.

Over the next couple of days, I could have wept. Each time I looked at my trousers, I wished I could turn back time – then I came up with a plan. I worked out that, if I went into the NAAFI shop and tried on a pair of the exact same trousers in the fitting room, I could replace them with my stained ones. I convinced myself it wasn't theft. After all, I told my conscience, the shop already had the money for a pair of trousers, all I was doing was swapping some over. The next morning, the first day of the weekend, I put my plan into action. My heart was thumping as

I left the changing room wearing the clean trousers, and hung up the oil-stained ones on the rail. I hurried for the door, but a combination of bad luck, looking guilty, and a sharp-eyed shop assistant meant that a hand was placed on my shoulder as soon as I stepped outside.

I was caught.

Wearing the new trousers and with the soiled ones in the hands of the shop assistant, I sat waiting while the Military Police were called. It may seem like an overreaction to have involved them, but official discipline was tight for Army kids; even the slightest misdemeanour could result in the big guns being brought in to teach you a lesson, and stealing – which was how my actions were perceived – was not seen as minor.

My heart was pounding and the sweat was pouring down my back as I waited for them. The irony was that this time I wasn't trying to draw attention to what was happening to me; I didn't mean to steal and I didn't mean to get caught deliberately, I just wanted my trousers to be nice for the school disco and to avoid upsetting Mum through her knowing that I had ruined one of the few things she had ever bought for me. However, once the Military Police came, gave me a stern talking to, and got me to change back into my own trousers, I was taken home, where I had no idea what would happen. As Mum was still in hospital, the policemen spoke only to Dad. I was terrified that, after the Glenda and Holly business, he would punish me his way. I sat there while the policemen told him how disappointed they were that I had done this, and watched as he

111

shook his head, looking for all the world as if he was as disappointed in me as they were.

'Well, Harry,' one of them said, as he stood up to go, 'we'll leave this with you. Now, young Tracy, we're hoping this will be a lesson to you – bad actions are always, *always*, found out, do you hear me?'

I nodded. I heard him, but I knew he was talking rubbish. If bad actions were always found out, he'd be taking my dad away rather than giving me a lecture.

I stayed sitting in the living room while Dad showed them to the door. I was resigned to something happening; I just didn't know what it would be. Dad sank into his chair and lit a cigarette. Sucking the smoke through his teeth, he narrowed his eyes at me.

'Well,' he said. 'Well, well, well. Who's a naughty girl, then?'

'I didn't mean anything bad by it!' I blurted out. 'It wasn't really stealing – I just wanted to change them. Really, Dad, I wasn't trying to shame you, really I wasn't.'

He sat quietly while I worked myself up into a frenzy. I don't know why I was so upset. I guess it must have been a combination of Mum being in hospital again, the fear when I got caught, the anger at myself that I had put myself in a vulnerable position with him again, and the knowledge that he now had something else to hold over me.

After a while, he said, 'I don't suppose we have to tell Mum, do we?'

I didn't feel relief.

'Please don't hurt me,' was all I could say.

He smiled, playing the moment for as long as he could.

'I won't tell Mum, but you remember in the future that I could tell her *any time* I want, so you be good, OK? No more fucking police at the door EVER again, you hear? Now fuck off out of my sight!'

It was the best I could have hoped for, but I knew I would pay.

Gary had seen the Military Police car leaving. He ran up the stairs just as I was going into my own room.

'Were the police here for you, Tracy?' he asked.

I nodded and told him why – I don't know why I confided in him, given he had never looked out for me before. Perhaps I still harboured the hope somewhere inside that, as my brother, Gary would be my ally. As I was telling him all about it, Dad came up behind us and said to Gary, 'I don't think your mother needs to know about this, do you? She's ill enough without any more worries, so keep your mouth shut, you hear?'

Neither the shop nor the Military Police took further action. The police said that the 'incident' would now be on my record, which they also said was now becoming a 'long list' due to the previous incident of shoplifting with Holly and Glenda, as well as the fire-starting. The NAAFI said that I was no longer allowed to enter the shop unless I was accompanied by an adult. Dad tried to use it against me as much as he could. Once Mum had returned home, he was always taunting me, saying things like, 'Well, I wonder if there's anything I should be mentioning to your mum?' It was just something else he could use to control me. This

113

went on for months, but I was getting older and I was getting sick of it all. There was one day I remember very clearly. Dad had come into my room while I was reading and started to touch me.

'Get away, get off me!' I said bravely.

'How dare you speak to me like that!' he replied. 'Have you forgotten everything? Have you forgotten what your behaviour can do to your mother?'

'No – no, I know all that, I know all that!'

'Well then – how would you feel if she knew about a certain incident in the NAAFI as well?' he threatened.

'Well, tell her then!' I snapped, completely fed up with his constant pawing at me and the way I never felt safe or free in my own home. I was becoming braver and rebelling more, and by saying this, I hoped to call his bluff, even though my stomach was churning.

'I might, I might very well do that,' he hissed. 'Just you remember – I could tell your mother any time.'

As he said those words, something flashed through my mind. *Yes, and I could tell her any time too*, I thought. There had been a creeping realisation (even if it was often subconscious) that this would happen. I *would* tell, I would; I just had to choose my time and be strong enough to deal with the repercussions, because there would certainly be more fallout than I could even imagine.

The incident with the trousers gave me time for reflection about everything that was going on with Mum, as much as what was going on with Dad. I recalled that, while waiting for the police in the NAAFI, it was Mum and her

114

reaction which was foremost in my mind. Perhaps that's because I knew what Dad would do – he would threaten me and continue to abuse me. I wasn't used to that as such, I would never get used to it, but he was predictable now. Mum always seemed to be able to find new ways to hurt me, and the very fact that I had got into trouble simply through trying to avoid causing her any distress was important. She had done so little – just bought me a pair of trousers – but it had been hugely significant, because it was the act of a normal mother towards a normal daughter in a normal relationship, and, as such, it was laden with more meaning than it actually should have been. There was a part of me that realised this. If we hadn't been só dysfunctional, I wouldn't have been in charge of the house, I wouldn't have been so disproportionately delighted at the buying of the trousers, and I would have simply said to Mum that they had been messed up rather than get myself into such a pickle.

These thoughts went through my mind during the days and weeks following my arrest. Why was I forced to protect Mum from what I did and from what Dad did all the time? It only resulted in me feeling even more disheartened, scared and unloved. Maybe *if* I had told her about the trouser incident, Dad wouldn't or couldn't have held it against me. Maybe *if* I had told her that I was scared, she would have asked me why, and it could all have come pouring out? That, for me, was the dream scenario. I so wished that, after an honest comment or remark from me, Mum would one day ask all the questions I desperately wanted to answer. If she did, then I could persuade myself that I hadn't told, not really. I could persuade myself that it was her love, her care, her maternal attention which had finally noticed that something was wrong and then – what a dream! – Mum would fix it all.

I constantly wondered about her reaction. Would she believe me? What would she do? Would she hold me, take me away from it all, say she was sorry, promise that we would be together and she would keep me safe forever? How would she react? Would she turn into the mother I needed, the mother I had always needed, rather than the mother she had been all of my life? I turned these questions over in my mind constantly. I wasn't quite ready to find out the answers – but I was getting there.

I don't think Dad or Gary did ever directly tell Mum about the NAAFI theft, but the fact that I had spilled everything to my brother didn't help me one little bit, as he told all the kids on the school bus. The following week on the bus to school, Patrick Gregory shouted at me, 'Oi, Tracy! What do we call you now, instead of second-hand Rose? Have you gone from rags to riches or riches to rags?'

The bus became the focus of so much dread for me. The other kids had a vague awareness of what was going on with Mum's illness; they certainly knew that she was often in hospital and that she often had ulcers on her legs. I guess they picked up things from their own parents, particularly their mums, and Gary would tell them stuff too. One time on the bus, after she had been readmitted to hospital, an older child started joking about and asking who was looking after us that day. All the other mums took turns at being a bus escort but mine never did. A new boy who had only been there for a couple of months turned to me and asked why my mum never took a turn.

'She's ill,' I said, trying to avoid going into too much detail.

'With scabies!' shouted another kid.

The bus erupted with laughter and they all turned on me.

'Your mum's got scabies!'

'Your mum's a scabby bag!'

'Your mum's covered in scabs and she stinks!'

I was so angry – and embarrassed – by this, and my only reaction was to verbally lash out.

'Fuck off!' I shouted at them all. 'Just fuck off! You shut up about my mum – just shut up, you've got no idea, any of you, no fucking idea!'

They were quiet for a moment, shocked at the ferocity of my response, but the ringleaders soon realised that this was a way to wind me up, so it went on for the rest of that week, the cries of 'Your mum's got scabies!' flung at me throughout each journey. By the time we got on the bus that Friday afternoon, I was at breaking point.

'Why's your mum not here then?' asked one girl. 'She's out of hospital, I saw her at the NAAFI – have her scabs not healed up?' she giggled. She was right. Mum was home, but she didn't do the school run out of choice, rather than due to illness. It was what normal mums did, caring mums, and she had no interest in anything like that.

When an older lad came right up to me, shoved his face into mine and hissed, 'Scabby – just like your mother!' before sitting down, laughing, I kicked him right out of the seat. Standing over him, half his size, I was ready to beat the living daylights out of him, until Gary pulled me off.

As soon as we got back, my brother ran in to Mum to tell her what had happened.

'Is this right?' she asked. 'Is he telling the truth, Tracy?'

I nodded, reluctantly, bracing myself for the battering that would surely come.

'Sorry,' I muttered. 'I won't do it again.'

'Well,' she huffed and puffed. 'I hope you will! Nasty little children calling me names – they have no idea what I go through, no idea the troubles I have. You did well, Tracy.'

I was stunned.

'Did I?' I asked, confused.

'Of course. It was very brave of you, standing up for your poor mother like that when I'm too weak to do it for myself. Bullies. Yes, you did well – and you did right to tell me,' she went on, hugging Gary, who was, of course, the perfect child for relaying the story, much more than I was for being 'brave'.

I was, naturally, delighted that I had done something to gain Mum's approval. Her state of delight didn't last though – by the time I had my next fight, she was back to being horrified by my actions. What no one knew was that my outbursts of verbal and physical violence always tended to come after episodes of abuse. If Dad did what he did to me one night, I could guarantee that I would, in turn, take it out on someone on the bus the next day. I wonder how often that happens? How often are the violent or disruptive or bullying children the ones who are experiencing horrors at home? Would it be a huge leap for adults in positions of authority to start asking these questions themselves? I don't think so, but I do wonder if anyone would be prepared for the torrent of revelations that might be unleashed.

Mum's reaction to that particular incident on the bus was unpredictable, and I often thought that her unpredictability was, perversely, the only predictable thing about her. When I think back to my childhood, and with the hindsight I have gained as an adult, I can now see that her way of showing her feelings towards me were also wrong, just like Dad's, albeit in a different way. When I was fighting for *her*, it was fine – when I was fighting for myself, or as a reaction to what was being done to me, I was a horrible little girl, a troublemaker and an embarrassment.

I was finally beginning to understand that a child shouldn't have to vie for their parents' attention. The fact that it had taken so long for this to dawn on me was another indicator of just how twisted my life was. I was beginning to realise that I had to face up to a horrible truth – maybe Mum just didn't love me. I was starting to rebel against Dad, but the hope that Mum would protect me was also beginning to fade. In fact, I started to detach my feelings from Mum too. Life was pretty awful, but it had been for so long that I barely knew anything different.

The whole experience of bussing every day was symbolic of how much I hated secondary school. I had enjoyed my primary school years in many ways – to some extent it had been a safe haven as the situation at home worsened – but this was different. I loved to be taught and wanted to learn, but being a loner and with so many problems to hide left me wishing that I didn't have to go to school at all. I know that the teachers questioned my behaviour and my work but they didn't seem concerned enough to find out the real reason or whether they could help in any way. I have tried to work out why that was the case – surely a lot of people go into teaching not just to impart knowledge but also to help children? If so, then why did no one ever notice anything? Even at the most basic level, why didn't they do something about the most obvious problem, which was that I smelled? Gary tried to mask the smell of dirty washing with Dad's Old Spice aftershave, but it didn't work – the only thing that did work for him was that he would threaten to batter anyone who called him names. I didn't have that option with the bigger kids, so I was resigned to smelling and being called names as a result.

Mrs Woods, my English teacher, was the only person at school to ever pick it up. She was an incredibly tall woman, lanky and thin, with a mass of bright red hair that hung in a sheet down her back. She was very nice and cheery, and she got a lot of respect from the kids; she was the only teacher who didn't hit any of us. The most punishment she ever gave out was lines and even that option was rare for her. One day, she pulled me aside and asked me why my clothes were sometimes smelly. She said that other kids in the class were aware of the smell. I shrugged my shoulders and told her I didn't know the reason.

'Is your mum having trouble drying your clothes?' she asked, kindly.

'My mum isn't home – she's in hospital again,' I told her, wondering whether this would be the moment when someone finally asked the questions I was so desperate to answer.

'Well, is your dad having problems?' Mrs Woods asked. 'Doesn't he dry the clothes outside?'

'No, Miss,' I explained. 'I do the washing when Mum isn't there and I'm not allowed to hang them outside.'

'You? You do all the washing? Surely not! I'm sure you mean you *help* your dad do it, Tracy – never mind, I'm sure he does his best, poor man. Now, stop exaggerating and run along to your next class.' And with that, she dismissed me.

I did as I was told, but as I ran down the corridor, I called back, 'I'm not exaggerating! I do it! I do it all on my own! I do everything!' But she said nothing. She may have been a lovely woman, but she had completely missed a child's cries for help. I managed to get some perfume from a friend and I started to use it to cover the smell. No more was said about it, but I think now that maybe if I hadn't been able to cover it up and the smell had become even worse, would they have looked into the conditions at home? This is so often the way of the abuse survivor – we look at ourselves constantly and wonder, what should I have done? What did I do wrong to make it all happen and why didn't

I stop it? Blaming yourself is all too easy, even when you know it was never your fault. I have looked back on those times and wondered – should I have made the smell worse? Should I have given up completely on any attempts at hygiene? Should I have given them all more clues?

But I did try, I did give clues, and still no one looked. At one point, Mrs Woods asked us to write a rhyming poem for homework, with the theme of 'rain.'

I remember that my poem began:

> *A child stands and watches the heavy rain*
> *Her head pressed against the window pane*
> *Neither thinking or talking just a blank stare*
> *Her heart heavy and sad and no one even aware*

Mrs Woods gave me back my jotter and said, 'how very profound for one so young! It's very good though, Tracy – an A plus for you!' She didn't hear or see a cry for help within the poem, and she didn't add it to any concern she had for the stench I created in the room. I think, more than anything, I would have loved for a woman to save me. I didn't trust men – how could I? – and I desperately wanted someone to love me and care for me in the way my own mother did not. When Mrs Woods didn't see anything, it was another blow.

There were some bright moments at school however – I loved art, and was never happier than when I was sketching or painting. My art teacher loved Pink Floyd and would get the pupils to paint copies of their record covers and posters. The main ones I remember were *A Saucerful of Secrets* and *Dark Side of the Moon* – I really tried to do well with these to curry favour. We also worked on our own projects and I have no doubt that my sketches, if done today, would be called disturbing to say the least, yet nothing was ever said to me about them. Some of my drawings, for example, depicted gravestones, coffins, a girl sitting on her own in a field with other children playing on the far side of her; there were always dark images and links to loneliness, fear and death. My projects were always just marked and given back to me without any comment.

By this point, I was fighting frequently, in the playground and in corridors, and I had also started to play truant. This resulted in me getting quite a few conduct cards. The first of the conduct cards began just three months after I started secondary school; I got it for fighting and it was quickly followed by one for truancy and then one more a few days later for fighting again. This third card in the space of a month resulted in me being given sessions with a social worker.

The fights I got into at school were usually with boys. When we were caught fighting we would both be sent to the headmaster's office. He would take us into his room individually but all of us seasoned 'bad kids' knew what was coming. The boy would get a whack across the palm of their hands with a chequered slipper with a foamed back (a lot like the Burberry check). When it was my turn, the head would always say, with a sad shake of the head, that I wasn't really a bad girl, so why would I be constantly getting myself into trouble? My only interactions with the opposite sex were with my dad, who sexually and physically abused me, my brother, who revelled in the favouritism he received and who never once stood up for me, and with my classmates, who taunted me daily. I hated all boys now.

In the whole eighteen months I was at that secondary school, I only had one fight with a girl and this was because Gary had instigated it. This girl, Tamsin, was known as the school bully. She was two years older than me and she didn't need much encouragement to pick on people. Gary was passing us in the corridor one day and he hit Tamsin on the back with his tennis racket. When she turned around, he said it was me. The fight was interrupted by a teacher and yet again I was sent to the headmaster's office; he seemed surprised that I had been in an altercation with a girl this time, but still shook his head sadly and said that he didn't believe I was bad.

I wasn't so sure.

If I wasn't – why did bad things happen to me? If I wasn't bad, why did no one care about any of it, turning a blind eye to all of the clues, all of the signs? I had been let down by my doctor, by my teacher, by the police, and by my brother. I was running out of people to turn to.

CHAPTER 7

TROUBLED

When we returned from Northern Ireland, Mum made contact with Agnes again. She was so pleased to see us all, I even got a big cuddle from her! She said I had changed and was becoming a big girl. 'A pretty one, too,' she told me, with a smile.

Mum's reply was instant: 'A big bloody nuisance more like.'

'I don't believe that for a minute,' said Agnes. 'You were always a good girl, Tracy. Has she changed, Valerie?'

'Christ, no,' said Mum. 'She's always been a pain in the arse. I'll tell you later, Agnes.'

We headed off, but I was confused yet again – what had I done now?

I next saw Agnes about a week later. When she asked if I was coping with moving schools again, I simply shrugged and said, 'I guess.' I was wondering what lies Mum had been spinning about me, and I felt uncomfortable. I'd always felt at ease with Agnes, but if Mum had been spinning warped tales to her about my behaviour, I would be labelled in whatever way she chose, with no way to defend myself.

Agnes went on to say that she'd thought a lot about me while we'd been away, that I had always had an air of unhappiness about me before the move and that I seemed to be a troubled child. In my young mind, I took 'troubled' to mean I was a troublemaker or always in trouble; I can see now that I had misconstrued her meaning, but back then her words cut me incredibly deeply, and I felt an intense sense of hurt. I had always felt Agnes was on my side but, having been through so much and with no one else to turn to, it now felt as if she was writing me off too.

'I'm not a troublemaker!' I shouted. 'I thought you liked me?'

I ran home sobbing, leaving Agnes open-mouthed at my outburst. Agnes told Mum about our little talk and when Mum approached me, her only concern was how I had embarrassed her and been rude to her friend. I told her that I wasn't a troubled child – I was a good girl! Mum must've realised at that point that I had misunderstood the difference between 'troubled' and 'trouble', but she let me go on thinking it meant I was bad. To explain the difference to me would have meant acknowledging the fact that something was making me unhappy; instead she buried her head in the sand.

It was all getting too much. I was at an age where I might very well have been rebelling anyway, and the amount of stuff in my head was unbearable. I wondered how many other little girls were being abused. Dad had said that it happened a lot, that it was normal and that I shouldn't question it, but I *did* have questions. Why did no one else seem to hate it the way I did? How did they manage to go on with their lives so well? What did they have that I didn't, which made it possible for them to laugh and make friends while their dads were abusing them too? The way in which my father messed with my mind as well as my body made these questions torture. His messages were being reinforced by what I was asking myself. If I couldn't cope with what was happening, but other girls could, then that simply reinforced how bad I was, how weird and unnatural. I should surely be able to deal with this – after all, everyone else did. When Mum would go into hospital, I would search my memory for a clue as to what I had done – or not done – to facilitate her illness. If she went into hospital even when Dad had been abusing me, I would think it was because I had said some-thing in the wrong tone, or been cheeky. Perhaps I hadn't been quick enough to go to my room, maybe I hadn't washed properly as he watched. There was always some-thing that I could blame myself for, and in doing so I played into his hands one hundred per cent. In time, I would blame myself for that too, because there is no one more likely to think badly of themselves than a child who is being abused. If you're told you're shit for long enough, you'll believe it – and I was a firm believer in how disgust-ing I was.

I could never predict what Dad was going to do exactly or when it was going to happen, but I was beginning to realise that he could always find some sort of justification for his behaviour. I remember one day, walking past him as he sat on his chair, when he kicked my legs away from me. I fell flat on my face. He rose up from his chair and stood over me as I cried.

'Why did you do that?' I asked, through the tears. 'What have I done wrong now?'

'I'm your dad! I can do what the fuck I like – you hear me?' he replied.

That always seemed to be his reasoning.

He was my dad – he didn't need any other excuse for what he did.

I managed to get through a couple of days without being hit after that, but one night after school he called me into his bedroom. Mum was, obviously, in hospital and I had come to dread the sound of his voice calling my name from that part of the house.

When I got there, he said, 'Tracy – Mum's not looking too good, don't you think?'

I was past caring some days. I didn't know what to think – I did all he asked, and she still got ill.

'I think that maybe you've not been as good as you could be – what do you think?'

I shrugged my shoulders.

'You cheeky little bitch!' he said. 'Fuck off – you've got no idea, really no fucking idea at all.'

I went to my room, delighted to have been sent away.

I know now that what he really wanted was for me to collude in the abuse, to be his 'little whore', to say that I loved it, and to remove all guilt from the whole business. Sometimes he could get past the indifference I showed to him, but sometimes it really ticked him off, and I escaped.

A few nights later, when Mum was back home, I was asleep when I felt his hand on my shoulder, roughly shaking me awake. It must have been well after midnight, as I had definitely been asleep for some time, and there was no other sound in the house, so Mum and Gary must have been the same way. The room was in darkness and he didn't put the light on; he had woken me from sleep before, sometimes turning on my bedside lamp, sometimes not. I think I hated it more when the light was on and he stared at me in places which cut me deep with shame.

As I lay there, still sleepy, he said nothing, but lifted up my nightdress. I waited for him to touch me but he didn't. Instead, after a few moments, he told me to do it myself.

'No,' I whispered. 'I don't want to.'

'Do it,' he said. He didn't sound angry, he wasn't pleading, he was just telling me what to do as calmly as if he had said that I should take my shoes off, or be careful when I crossed the road. It was as if he thought he was making a perfectly normal request.

I tried to turn away from him, but he grabbed my hand and twisted me round again.

'You heard me, Tracy – do it, touch yourself. Touch yourself *there.*'

I shook my head; even in the darkness he must have known that I was doing this as he got cross and hissed, 'I'm telling you what to do – so do it!'

Still holding on to my hand, he placed it between my own legs.

'Go on – you'll like it,' he said, as I started to cry. 'Do it, Tracy – it's fun. I'm telling you, do it.'

With his use of the word 'fun', I cried louder.

'For fuck's sake, stop snivelling. I'm only trying to make you feel good!' he snarled. With that he threw the bed covers over me and stormed out.

'What's wrong with her?' I heard Mum ask. 'What's going on?'

'Nightmare,' Dad replied. 'Just a nightmare, Valerie, she's all right now.'

I lay there, still, and listening intently for any further sounds from their bedroom. Even after all this time, a small part of me harboured the hope that Mum might get up and come in to check on me herself. She didn't come. As I waited for sleep to arrive and block out for a few hours the horror of what he had just tried to make me do, I heard nothing but silence.

I have asked myself the same question so many times – what made Mum the way she was? I have pieced together as much of her background as I can, but it doesn't really help, there are no big events which jump out at me saying THIS! This is why she hated you! As far as I know, Mum's childhood appears to have been uneventful and normal. She never told us stories about her childhood or the games she played. She never spoke about any boyfriends. She didn't appear to have come from an abusive home. She says she met Dad at a dance, they courted for a short time, then married. Mum never told me romantic stories or tales which engaged me as a child; it just all seemed very ordinary, so there were no clues there for me when I tried to unpick it all. Sometimes, I would hear little bits from the rest of the family, but I had no way of knowing what was true and what was passed-down gossip. My paternal grandmother liked to tell anyone who would listen that Mum had got pregnant to some Australian swimmer, and then married Dad to save face. Was she happy with Dad? I don't think she was terribly *un*happy, but he was a jealous man, and she must have felt constrained by that at times.

Mum's father died before she married, and when she left home, to set up her own life with Dad, she had no contact with her own mother ever again, not even returning for the funeral. I don't know why, but I guess that does show she could be cold to more people than just her daughter. She had little contact with her siblings either, she never phoned them or wrote letters – it was as if she wanted no part of that life. If there were photographs of her as a child, or of her wedding, Gary and I never saw them.

Shortly after Gary was born, the new little family moved from Scotland to Malta on a posting. Later on, I would hear Mum tell friends in Germany and Northern Ireland that she was lonely there and had always felt isolated. They were there for a few years. I remember one story she told Gary that took place in Malta. I must have been about seven when I heard this tale (sometimes I can only work out what age I was by thinking of 'before the abuse started in Germany' or 'after the abuse started in Germany' – these are the markers of my life). Mum said that Gary had been poorly and the heat was worrying her, as she thought it would push his temperature still higher. I was only a baby at the time, and sleeping in a cot. Mum wanted to open the window in the room we were sharing, so she took my mosquito net and put it over his bed, leaving me completely unprotected. Unsurprisingly, I became covered in bites and actually had to be hospitalised. When Mum told this story to Gary, with me sat there listening, she seemed to think it was hilarious.

'Covered in them, she was!' she giggled. 'I could hardly see a patch of clear skin – they'd had a good feast on her all right, but you . . . you didn't have a single bite on your body,' she told Gary, leaning over to give him a kiss on the top of his head. He shrugged her off as usual and seemed completely uninterested, but I wanted to know more.

'What did they say at the hospital, Mum?' I asked.

'That you were a pain in the arse!' she replied.

'No, really – what did they say?' I asked again.

'That was the full medical diagnosis,' she said. 'And it was fatal – couldn't be changed.' She smirked at me, always happy if she had managed to get another dig in. I was speechless – even then it seemed odd that a mother would take a net from a little baby to put on her older child, effectively choosing which one she wanted to protect. Surely she could have got another one for Gary, or even for me once she had given him mine? No, it appeared that once she had protected him, I was disposable. This showed to me that, even from the outset, Mum had been cold towards me. Had she suffered from postnatal depression? Maybe – those sorts of things weren't really spoken about back then, but even if she had, why had it lasted so long? Why did it last forever?

As I was getting older, I thought my relationship with Mum might change. After all, I reasoned, her stays in hospital were becoming less frequent, and she seemed to be getting a little better, even though the doctors still hadn't worked out what was wrong with her. I wondered whether she might like me more once I was past the stage of being a very small child. If I was as annoying and clinging as she said, surely that would pass? I didn't really think we would ever be one of those mother–daughter pairs who were more like friends than family, but I did wonder whether she would start to like me more. She never did.

When Mum was ill or in hospital, I tried to keep the house tidy, but it was never as good as the way she did it, according to Dad, and he let me know. Once Mum was feeling better, she would do the house to her 'standard'. As far as I knew – and from what he told me – Dad never let her know just how much I was taking on. He would just say that we 'muddled through'. I certainly never got any praise for what I did. I did tell Mum that I had done the washing and made the beds, but Dad would always say I was exaggerating. That fitted in with what she thought of me anyway, as she would often call me 'Walter Mitty'. If I had a bruise from Dad holding me down during the abuse, I would, in the past, make up a story for how I had got it. However, once I was about twelve, I decided to test the waters. One day, when she grabbed me by the arm and said, 'How did you do that then, you clumsy little cow?' I told her the truth.

'It was Dad,' I said.

'What are you talking about – do you mean he hit you?'

I shook my head.

Mum knew he hit me, she was often there, and it didn't bother her in the slightest.

'Well,' she said, ignoring the fact that I had shaken my head, 'if he hit you, he must have had good reason. You must have deserved it.'

'He didn't hit me,' I said.

She started to walk away.

'Don't you want to know how I got it?' I asked. 'You were the one who brought it up.'

'Oh, shut up, you little Walter Mitty!' she shouted back at me. 'Always wanting attention, always exaggerating things.'

She didn't really want to know anything. Dad would often admit that he had clouted me, but if there was ever really severe bruising, he would blame Gary. He knew that was one person who would never be punished, so Mum would simply drop the topic if he said my brother had been punching me. He was never confronted, I was never consoled. That was just the way things were, that was just the story of my life.

CHAPTER 8

THE PIECES OF MY LIFE

When Dad would knock me about and call me names, there was such venom in his voice, as if he was taking out some unresolved anger on someone else, only using me as the target. I do think he was often releasing something on me, something in his past, something unnamed, something that actually had nothing to do with me, but which I bore the brunt of. To begin with, I did nothing to deserve it, nothing at all; but as I got older, and more unhappy, I became a naughty child, I accept that. I stole, I skived school, I set fires, I was cheeky, I was defiant; by then, if he wanted to, he could justify his violence against me by saying that I needed to be disciplined. But I was that sort of child for a reason.

I remember him beating me once because he was so annoyed at Mum being taken into hospital again. 'Always down to me!' he shouted as he hit me. 'Always up to me to fucking cope with you and your brother, you little bastard!'

I think that, even if he hadn't been the sort of man to sexually abuse me, I would still have been beaten. The look on his face, the way that he seemed to be in another place while he was doing it, makes me feel that he was just wired that way. I see scenes from my life and I want to reach into them and save that child, I want to save Tracy. At the beginning, I was his good little girl, and good little girls like me never, never told the secret. My skin crawls when I see another scene in which he's telling me that I'm a *little darling, Daddy's girl, baby doll, prossie*. I see him laughing when I look confused, and he goes on to say that I'm *Daddy's little prostitute*.

I have a knot in my stomach when I think of how he used me to replace my mother, the way in which he wanted me to take on all of her roles – looking after Gary, cooking, cleaning, doing the laundry and, of course, in the bedroom. I want to scream at the little girl in that memory to tell, to shout, to let someone know – but it's too late, I can't step back into the past and make things different. 'Normal' life went on.

Although Dad was exempt from most Army exercises due to Mum's illness, once a year, sometimes twice, he would do a two-week one. It was much less than the other men, but he still made a huge fuss of it, acting as if he was terribly important and that the safety of the entire Western world depended on him! I remember him preparing to go on exercise on one occasion. At the same time, Gary was to leave for a skiing trip. Mum was getting very stressed as she had a shopping trip to London planned, and kept saying, 'What about me?' every time Dad or Gary mentioned that they would be off soon.

Dad told her that if she wanted to go, she would have to take me too, but, either way, to make up her mind quickly. Mum was stuck. She desperately wanted to go on this shopping splurge (for herself and Gary), but hated the idea of being 'landed' with me.

Eventually, she decided that she'd take me.

'I bloody suppose she'll have to trail along after me too, as usual,' she complained. 'She doesn't deserve it though – do you hear me?' she asked, even though I'd been in the room all the time. 'You're coming but I don't even want to know you're bloody there, and don't go thinking this is some treat for you. I'm taking you because I've got no bloody choice!'

I was under no illusions that Mum (and Dad) thought I deserved such a treat – my behaviour had been getting steadily worse by this point – but I would still rather have been with her than not. Though she'd been in hospital over the summer months, on her return Mum had perked up a lot, hence the shopping trip. There were lots of women going, all from the bingo. On the day of the trip, I was all wrapped up as it was bitterly cold. Mum said that it would be even colder when we hit our destination – Dover to begin with, before the capital. It seemed like a really adventurous trip to me as I rarely went anywhere. We all got picked up from the NAAFI and went on the same green bus that took us to school each day. A couple of older girls tagged along too, but they couldn't be bothered with me, as they were about fifteen or sixteen and, as I was only twelve, they saw me as a kid. They giggled the whole way, whispering about 'civvy' boys and wondering if they were nicer than Army 'brats'. The bus took us to the ferry, about two hours away, and I couldn't help but feel excited. Mum didn't pay me much attention on the way there, she pretty much stayed with her friends, so I tried to look as if I was perfectly happy with my own company and kept to myself.

When we got on the ferry, she settled down with the other women to spend the whole crossing playing bingo. They'd brought all their own supplies and she grudgingly gave me a card to fill in when one of the other women suggested that I could play too. I replayed it for most of the trip as I only had one, but I didn't win anything. It was nice to be included though, even if someone else had managed it on my behalf, and Mum had only given it to me to shut me up.

It was an uneventful crossing, but I was apprehensive. I remembered a previous trip from Larne to Stranraer during terrible weather. The thunderstorm during that voyage had caused us to be tossed about, and people around me had even been vomiting, so I dreaded what would happen on this one. Mum knew I was scared and why, but she did nothing to soothe me or calm me down. She just called me a 'nuisance' and said that I was a terrible burden to her. Once I realised it was quite calm, I was able to get a little bit excited about the prospect of shopping in London, and when we arrived for the train all I could think was that it was truly amazing just how much bingo these women could play! They never stopped – from the base to the ferry, from the ferry to London, it was just bingo, bingo, bingo. Some of the women did a fair bit of drinking too, but not Mum, she just wanted to play. As always, I was seen and not heard.

On the train, Mum looked very tired. She said that she wasn't feeling too well and she certainly had that funny colour about her that she always got prior to falling ill. Six months earlier, she had been a guinea pig for a new drug and she often said it made her feel so weak. I could hear her saying, 'I feel so tired,' over and over again. Everyone was having a great time, and I was the only one really paying attention to her, but she kept pushing me away, saying that I should stop bothering her. When we got off, she passed out almost immediately. All the other mums had started to go their own ways when we got off, so it was really just me who was with her. I shouted out and, luckily, one of her friends looked back and saw Mum on the floor. She called for help and I waited until the ambulance arrived, watching in horror as they checked over her unconscious body. I didn't know Mum's friend, who introduced herself as Rose, but she seemed like a nice lady.

Rose spoke to the ambulance men and briefly gave them a rundown regarding what she knew of Mum's illness. She told them that Mum had previously been admitted to hospital many times in Germany and that she had been ill for years. After they had all discussed Mum, Rose turned to me, took my hand and said, 'Right – let's go.'

'What?' I asked, confused. 'Where? Let's go where?'

'Back home,' answered Rose. 'I'll get you back to Germany and back to the safety of your dad.'

Mum was still unconscious when Rose took me away, saying that there was nothing I could do and that the professionals were in charge now. Bizarrely, we still went shopping – Rose's idea of getting me back home was to take me around London for two days while the bingo ladies continued with their outing. I don't remember much of the trip, as I was busy worrying about Mum and about what would happen when I got home, but I remember that Rose did look after me, never letting me out of her sight while we were there.

Dad had been contacted while all this was going on, and recalled from his exercise. He was waiting at the NAAFI when we returned.

'What have you done now?' were the first words he spoke to me when I got back.

All I could think was *Mum's in hospital and Gary isn't due home for another three days. What's he going to do to me if he has me all alone for that time?*

Of course, I knew exactly what he would do. There was no one to interrupt him, no one to unexpectedly stop him doing whatever he wanted. Gary went straight to his room when he got home later that week, and was so tired from his skiing trip that he didn't go out to see friends or play football for ages. I felt that his presence in the house protected me to some extent.

Mum returned home a couple of weeks later as if nothing had happened. She looked well. Not once did she ask how I was, what had become of me when she collapsed, or if I had been taken care of properly. Falling ill and having to be rushed back to Germany to be hospitalised didn't stop her from planning another trip. She decided about eight months later that we would go back to London, this time from Zeebrugge, so that she could buy Christmas presents. I wondered whether she wanted to make it up to me, whether she had planned all along for us to have some mother and daughter time, and had been disappointed herself that it had never happened.

'I'm looking forward to it, Mum,' I said.

'Well, I'm not,' she told me. 'Your dad's away that weekend and Gary wants to go camping – I only need you there in case I have a funny turn again. Christ knows why I bother – you're probably bringing all this bad luck on me anyway.'

My heart felt as if she had stabbed a knife into it. I was the one trying to keep her well! I was the one trying to keep her out of hospital! Every time Dad made me touch myself and said I would love it, I hoped it would keep Mum's pains away. When he wanted me to talk dirty so that he could masturbate, tell him that I needed to be 'fucked', that was for Mum. The thought that she believed I was 'bad luck' was like a slap in the face.

We went on the trip, and she kept well this time. There was no fainting, no call for ambulances, just bingo and shopping. She only bought things for herself and for Gary; I didn't get as much as a souvenir T-shirt. I wondered whether she was buying me anything on the sly for

Christmas, but on the way back, she said, 'I'll have to see if the charity shops have anything for you when I get a bit of a rest. I'm worn out from this trip but I suppose you'll whine if you get nothing from Santa.'

Was she joking? I smiled, hoping to avoid angering her as I always seemed to do.

'You look simple sometimes, do you know that?' she remarked. 'Don't go thinking I'm planning a surprise – you'll get whatever I can afford and be bloody grateful for it.'

She kept to her word. My Christmas gifts that year all had the unmistakeable aroma of charity shop about them, and were clearly second-hand. Gary, meanwhile, was presented with a pile of beautifully wrapped gifts, most of them from London, and a beaming mother who could not do enough for him. It was hard when I returned to school after the holidays and the other kids asked what I'd got. I just lied – I was good at that.

Mum's health worsened in the new year, and as summer approached she had to be taken back into hospital once more. This time, Dad decided that he couldn't look after me and Gary any more – it was decided that Gary, Dad and I would stay with family members in Scotland. My Auntie Dee took me in, while Dad took Gary to stay with someone else. Auntie Dee had four kids and was a wonderful mother, and I spent that entire summer being happy – happy to see what a normal family looked like, and even happier to be part of it. Dee adored them all and gave them so much attention and love. She loved me too, as did her husband

Freddie. It was a real eye-opener to watch them at close quarters, because most of my beliefs about how 'normal' families worked were either based on my limited interaction with Agnes, or imaginary. I couldn't believe how natural they all were with each other. There was no violence, no abuse, just love and laughter. That trip was a turning point for me.

When I got back to Germany, I couldn't stop thinking about Dee and her world. I wanted that. I was rebelling but not getting the reaction I wanted, which only drove me to find new ways of acting up. My behaviour had deteriorated to such an extent that I had now been assigned a social worker, Mrs Walker, to 'look after' me. If Dad had felt any worry about what the social worker might uncover about our family situation, he needn't have. To begin with I had seen her as a chance, an opportunity to be rescued – as a professional, surely she was trained to notice what I was going through, surely she would offer me an escape route? But she was less than useless. She made no attempt to get to the bottom of my behaviour, and I soon came to realise that all she saw was a naughty little girl who told lies. But I was reaching breaking point emotionally, and one day on our way to our usual 'session' carried out in a café over a lukewarm cup of tea, I decided it was now or never.

As we sat in her car, she asked me the same things she always did: how had my day been at school, had I had my conduct cards signed, and then the question I had been waiting for: did I think I could be a good girl? This was my opportunity. I felt my mouth go dry and my heart start pounding. I closed my eyes, took a deep breath and said: 'I know why I've been naughty.'

'Really?' she said, surprised by this admission and taking her eyes off the road briefly to glance at me. 'Why is that?'

'It's my dad, it's because my dad touches me. He's been touching me and hurting me and doing bad things for so long, and I just want it all to stop.' It was the least offensive thing I could say really – if I'd actually listed all of the things he had been doing and what he had forced me to do in return, I think she would have had a heart attack. As it was, she almost crashed the car.

'Don't say such terrible things, Tracy!' she shrieked. 'What an awful excuse to give for your appalling behaviour.'

'But, Mrs Walker,' I insisted, 'it's true, he does do things to me.'

'It's utterly ridiculous to even think of such a thing. Your father is right – you're a very bad girl indeed,' she told me.

Her response was appalling, personally and professionally. I had waited so long to tell someone and it was dismissed out of hand. The conversation was over and when we reached the café, she sat silently filling out her forms. She certainly never put it in her report because those documents went to my parents; I would have known if Mrs Walker had revealed what I'd told her.

*   *   *

How many opportunities had there been in the last seven years for someone to step in and pull me out of this nightmare? How many times had I been let down by the people who should have recognised the signs of abuse and asked me what was going on? Doctors, teachers, family friends. And now, my social worker too. Every day now seemed filled with despair; I felt alone, trapped and scared. I realised that things couldn't go on the way they were.

My thoughts were racing through my head: perhaps if I told Mum everything, she would come to my aid? She may not have been the mother I wanted or needed in the past, she may not want to spend any time with me; she may not love me the way she loved Gary. But I was desperate for Mum to acknowledge that something was troubling me – at that moment, I felt I had nothing left in my life but her. Surely not even she could turn her back on her own daughter once she knew of the abuse? It was all I thought of. I had made up my mind. I went through every scenario in my mind – how to tell her, when to tell her, what to tell her. When she got back from hospital, she seemed healthier than I could ever remember, and so I plucked up my courage one night, when Gary was at a sleepover and Dad was working.

She was sitting in the living room, watching the television. When I entered the room, she kept her eyes fixed firmly on the screen. 'Mum,' I began, trying to draw her attention away from her programme. 'I've got something I need to talk to you about . . . It's a bit difficult . . .'

'What have you been doing?' she snapped. 'Have you been messing with boys?' She immediately assumed I had been up to no good.

'No,' I said. 'I mean it's not that, but it's something like that. It's really hard to say, Mum . . .'

'Well, bloody try harder and hurry up, will you? I haven't got all night.' She did have all night – she was staying in and watching TV, not going out to bingo, much to her displeasure I imagine.

I hesitated at this point, desperate to turn around and run to my bedroom – terrified by the idea of telling Mum, yet terrified by the prospect of spending another day in this shameful silence.

'Mum, it's about Dad,' I said. I had no idea how to phrase this, how to shatter her world. How could I verbalise the terrible things he had done to me and made me do, the terrible things I had kept secret for so long? But I knew I had to – I had made it this far, I couldn't turn back now – so I took a breath and forced out the words: 'He's been doing things to me, Mum. He's been touching me in ways he shouldn't for years!'

There was a slight pause, a fraction of a second's silence. And then, 'Rubbish,' she said, still looking at the television.

I felt a wave of fear wash over me.

'It isn't rubbish, it's the truth. Since I was five, he's told me that I have to do these things to keep you out of hospital and that's why I have. I loved you so much, Mum, and I'd have done anything to make you well.'

148

She said nothing.

'Mum? Did you hear me? Did you hear what I said?'

'I heard it.'

'Mum! He raped me! Dad's been raping me!'

Turning to face me finally, standing up slowly as she did, she pointed her finger at me and met my gaze at last.

'*HE* is my husband. *YOU* are only my daughter. It's all lies. Go away.'

'But, Mum—' I wept.

'You've been told,' Mum said. 'You – *you* are just my daughter. You're nothing. *He* is my husband, and I will always stand by him.'

'But, Mum,' I continued, 'you don't know what he's been doing . . .'

'I do know you lie till you're blue in the face,' she snorted. 'And that you need to stop these lies, stop these stories. Tracy, you need to move on – no one cares.'

I was stunned. In all the scenarios, in all the ways I had played out this scene in my head, I had never seen this coming. Not this absolute complete and utter betrayal. As I fled to my room and lay on my bed, heartbroken and sobbing, I tried to make sense of her reaction. Surely the normal response would have been upset or tears? Some kind of outrage or horror at what she had just heard? Not this calm denial and the blaming of a child for telling lies. Did she know? Had she known for years?

I started to think of other parts of my life, putting together other pieces of the jigsaw. She had frequently ignored my bruises and she had ignored Agnes's concerns about me being a troubled child. She never questioned my unwashed state or wonder at my absolute terror of being left alone with men. But I started thinking about the other things, too: on days when Dad and I were alone and Mum had been out, she would always call out 'I'm home' or some other greeting when she returned. Then she would head straight to the kitchen to put the kettle on. Yet, when I was out with her and we returned home together, she wouldn't call out or head for the kitchen at all, she would go straight into the sitting room and sit down. Why did she change her behaviour when she knew Dad and I were home alone? She kept me away from her friends and their homes because Dad had laid down the law on this subject, but she could have still taken me when he was out – he would've been none the wiser. So why didn't she? Was she scared of what I might reveal to outsiders?

Looking back now, I think I truly gave up on Mum at that point. If she couldn't love or protect me for the first twelve years of my life, I sure as hell knew she wouldn't in the future. I never gave up the hope that things would turn out differently, but I think that was the moment I gave up on the dream that she would be the one to help me.

CHAPTER 9

BOARDING SCHOOL

Shortly after telling Mum – and being called a liar – something seemed to change in me. I think that the very act of putting the abuse into words brought this change about, even if no one believed me. I realised that I needed to get out of my own life and away from my family. I had to take charge of my future. I felt as if I was eighteen rather than thirteen, I felt as if I was at that stage in my life where everything gets assessed and decisions are made; but the sad truth was, I was still a child, even if I was a child who had never been allowed a childhood.

I felt like something had been set in motion. I think I had long known that as soon as I told someone, my life would change. I guess I was breaking the spell in a sense. All of Dad's lies and manipulations were shattered from that moment, because, in giving voice to what had happened, I was bringing the outside world into my private hell.

As an adult, of course I wondered why I hadn't said anything earlier, why I had continued Dad's charade of secrets and games. I've never been able to fully answer my own questions, but perhaps that's understandable. When you look at something through the eyes of an adult, and when you have escaped, it's impossible to be in that place from years before, when everything was so dark. When I wonder why I kept quiet, I do that as a grown woman, as a mother, as a businesswoman, as a competent, confident individual – not as a five-year-old; and, while the questions may be asked, I would never want to betray that five-year-old by saying that it was wrong to keep quiet for so long. I only did what I did because of the absolute control Dad had over me, and because of the unquestioning love I felt for Mum. Neither of those things – his control over me, my love for her – are there any more, so I can't judge myself on what I did when they were. I think every abuse survivor has to, somehow, come to the point where they have made a peace with themselves, no matter how uneasy that peace is. I was blamed and excluded and made to feel like dirt for so long – I try very hard not to keep doing all those things to myself, but it's hard. It's very hard.

I had no idea what was in store for me but it had to be better than the life I was living. I decided to run away, and confided in my friend Holly.

'Does your Dad ever hit you?' I asked her one evening.

'Why? Does yours?' she answered, immediately.

'Yes – yes, he does, and I'm really fed up with it,' I told her. I wanted to see what her reaction was, to work out whether I should go further and tell her what else he did, but she wasn't that interested.

'It's just what they do,' she said, 'best keep out of his way if you can – you can stay in our cellar tonight if you like?'

I was delighted by the offer, but the next day she assumed I would be going home.

'I thought you meant that I could stay here?' I said.

'Well – I did, but just for last night!' she replied.

'Holly, I need somewhere for longer, I need somewhere permanent,' I told her.

'Not here! You can't live in our cellar forever,' she gasped. 'So what if your dad is giving you a slap now and again? Plenty of them do – but you can't move out, you can't just leave home and move into ours! Anyway, they'll be much nicer to you now that you've shown them that you don't mind running away. They'll be worried and your dad will lay off you for a while, I bet.'

I knew that was not likely to be the case, but Holly made it clear that she couldn't hide me for any longer.

'You'll have to go, Tracy,' she told me, assertively. 'I don't want to get in trouble because you can't deal with your dad.'

I went to the house of another girl, this one called Gillian, and told her the same story. Again, I was only allowed to stay there for one night, so I went back to Holly's again.

'He's been here, he's been looking for you,' she informed me.

'Dad?' I asked, trembling.

'Of course your dad – who else?' said Holly. 'Your mum's ill again, you, Tracy, you've got to get home.'

153

All my determination faded away when I heard about Mum. I was still so worried about her, and rushed back home to see what had happened. A part of me did wonder if Dad was lying but, when I got home, Mum had indeed been taken to hospital. That night, as Dad abused me yet again, even more violently this time to punish me for running away, I knew that I needed to stand my ground. As soon as he left my room, I went back to Gillian's, where I had stayed the second night, and crept into her cellar without telling anyone. I was terrified in case I was caught and didn't go to school the next day, but just couldn't find the strength I needed to stay away forever. I seemed to be constantly wavering between deciding I needed to leave with no going back, and finding myself drawn there again because of Mum. Knowing that she was in hospital was killing me that day as I wandered around during school hours, hoping that no one would see me. I had nothing to help with distraction, and although I no longer believed that Dad's abuse of me was in any way linked to Mum's ill health, I still wanted to do all I could for her.

Eventually, I could bear my own thoughts no longer. I plucked up my courage and went home, needing to know how Mum was, needing to know that she was on the mend.

As soon as I opened the door, I heard her voice. She was back already.

'Mum?' I said, running into the living room to see her. 'You're home!'

'Of course I'm home – they kick me out as soon as they can these days,' she said, not making any move towards me

154

and even holding up her hands to keep me at a distance. 'In fact, I think they're sick of the sight of me. I hope you've been behaving yourself?' she said, narrowing her eyes at me, suspiciously.

I waited for Dad to tell her that I hadn't even slept in my bed, but he said nothing and she obviously had no idea. He raised his eyebrows at me and smiled, as if giving me a warning. I didn't know whether he had chosen not to tell her because he wanted to have that over me too, or whether he didn't think the information was important enough to bother her with. I guess, either way, he assumed I would be back.

'I'll make you a cup of tea, Mum,' I said, going into the kitchen. Dad was there in seconds.

'You put all thoughts of running away out of your mind, do you hear me?' he hissed. 'She'll get ill again if you do – it'll all be your fault.'

For the first time, I laughed in his face. 'Don't bother, Dad,' I said. 'I've worked that one out.'

I pushed him away and went to my room, slamming the door behind me. I think, more than anything, what hit me that night was that Dad was still using the same lies that he had used since I was five. He was so sure of himself, and so sure that I would always be his puppet, that he hadn't even bothered to change his story.

I grabbed my backpack and left. He had taken so much from me, but so had Mum. I would never get those years back again, I would never have a chance to build happy childhood memories, but I could start changing my life from this point on. It was time to start shouting and time to start standing up for myself. Neither parent had ever shown me love – not appropriate love – and now I had to finally learn how to be kind to myself, I was the only one I could rely on.

I knew that if the police found me they'd take me straight home again, so I decided to see if Holly would let me stay longer this time.

I knocked on her front door and hoped it would be her who opened it, but I wasn't in luck.

'Is Holly coming out?' I asked her mum, smiling and trying to look friendly. All the while, my stomach was churning as I just knew that I couldn't go back home, and I really needed Holly to come through for me.

When she appeared, I grabbed her by the hand and walked out onto the street.

'I can't go back, Holly!' I said. 'I can't go back there.'

'What's going on?' she asked. 'Is your dad being really horrible to you?

I didn't want to go into detail, so I just said things were 'getting worse'.

'My mum and dad are going out tonight,' Holly told me. 'You can sleep in the cellar, they won't check it when they get back, they'll be too drunk.'

That night I slept well, as if a huge weight had been lifted from me.

The next day Holly came down to visit me.

'You'll need to go,' she told me, nervously. 'Dad's going to be at home for a while and he'll find you, so you really need to get away.'

'Where? Where will I get away to?' I asked. 'I don't have anywhere to go.'

Holly was getting more and more agitated, but finally suggested that I could go to her auntie's house. The woman was on holiday, thus leaving a vacant cellar at her house, so I gratefully wrote down the address.

I spent the day there, cold and hungry, but at least safe. I tried to sleep but only managed to doze infrequently. However, after a few hours, just as night was falling, I must have dropped off, because the sound of footsteps coming down the stairs woke me. I prayed that Holly would have brought some food with her, but she'd brought something else . . . she'd brought my dad.

'I'm so sorry,' she whispered as she stood beside me with Dad smirking from the door. 'He came to our house and my dad told me that I had to say where you were if I knew what was good for me.'

I looked at her with tears in my eyes.

'It's only hitting,' she muttered. 'Everyone gets hit by their dad, you just have to put up with it.'

If I could have curled up on the floor and gone to sleep forever, I would have, but Dad was standing there, watching me with a look on his face as if to say, *don't even think about saying anything, don't even think about running. I've won. They believe me.* He was right, I was sure of it; he would have come across as the caring parent to Holly's family and I would, no doubt, be looking like a silly little girl running away for no good reason, causing trouble to a good man.

'Time to go home, Tracy,' Dad announced. 'Time to put an end to this silly nonsense.'

With that, he climbed the stairs out of the cellar; by the time I followed, he was waiting, standing alongside Holly's father. As I looked up, I could see the two men were not alone, they were not the only adults there.

There were also two Military Police officers.

In that moment, I was in two minds – were they the enemy or could they help me?

Dad continued to smirk, as he had done in the cellar.

'I don't think that you quite understand the conse-quences of your actions, Tracy,' he said in a voice that I think was meant to scare me and impress the others. 'You have caused a lot of trouble, a *lot* of trouble, and that can't be allowed to go unpunished.'

I could tell that he assumed I would be scared by the presence of the officers, but I wasn't – the more he spoke, the more I realised that I was relieved. I had made myself a promise to get out of this, and they could offer me a route.

'Do you hear me?' he continued. 'Do you understand how much damage you've done?'

'I hear you,' I said quietly. 'I hear you.'

I waited a moment – as did everyone else.

'I want to talk to them,' I announced, staring Dad in the face.

'Who?' he replied.

'I want to talk to the police officers.'

His face dropped before he regained his composure.

'Well, yes – they may very well want to talk to you at some point too. I would think that very likely actually – but let's get you home and you can think about your behaviour.' He made a move towards me, attempting to take my elbow with his hand. I pulled away.

'No,' I insisted. 'I want to talk to them now. I want to talk to you!' I said, more loudly in their direction.

They had been listening and one of them stepped forward. I'm sure Dad thought they would only see a girl who started fires, who ran away, who broke windows, who shoplifted, who caused criminal damage – but they must have seen something else. They must have seen a child who wanted something from them.

Staring coldly at Dad, one of them ushered me aside.

'I'm sorry,' he said, 'but we do need your dad to be here because of your age. Is that all right?'

'No, no it's not,' I muttered. 'I'm running away *because* of him, I'm getting into trouble *because* of him. Don't you see? He's behind it all and I can't have him here while I speak to you – while I tell you things.'

Dad was watching all of this but one of the Military Police officers was making sure he couldn't get any closer. I don't know what those guards sensed – or maybe they even had suspicions about Dad that were stronger than that – but they kept him away, and listened to me.

'What do you mean?' asked the one beside me.

I knew it was my last chance. If no one believed me now, they never would. Taking a deep breath, I told this complete stranger, a man who was, to all intents and purposes, on my dad's side, the things that had been kept inside me for so long.

'He's been abusing me. He's been doing it for years. My dad – my dad abuses me,' I said, quickly but with as much feeling as I could. 'Please help me,' I whispered.

And – to his eternal credit – he did.

Dad wasn't allowed in the car, despite his ranting and raving. The officers said nothing to me other than that they were taking me to Army headquarters and that Dad would follow in another car provided for him.

When we arrived, I felt everyone was looking at me. I have no objective way of knowing whether they were, but when an abused child finally talks, there is an awful lot of shame mixed up with the relief, even when someone finally listens. What did they all know, I wondered? Did they think I was dirty? Did they think I was disgusting for letting him do those things to me? I was informed that I was being taken to speak to the 'boss', a man called Commanding Officer Stewart. I had never met with or seen him before, and felt sick to my stomach that my future was in his hands. What sort of man was he, I pondered? A father? A good father? And, if so, what *kind* of good father – one like my dad, was he one of them?

I waited for two hours before he saw me. Perhaps he was getting as much information as he could, I didn't know, but I was shaking with fear by the time I was ushered in.

CO Stewart was tall, thin and very posh. He was also very gentle as he told me that he'd chatted with Dad, who had, predictably, denied everything. I wasn't surprised and expected now to be kicked out of the office and returned home. CO Stewart took me unawares by asking me why I had been playing up. When I told him it was to stop Dad abusing me, he looked quizzical, then asked, 'How would that stop it?'

I hadn't really thought of it before, but I realised that I had always assumed that if people saw me being so bad, they would ask why. The fact that no one had was beside the point; I had *thought* they would. I knew that they didn't care when I was smelly or neglected, when I was bruised or sad, but when I started damaging property they did notice me, just not in the right way, and they never did ask the questions they should have asked.

CO Stewart was quiet as he thought about all of this. He didn't shout at me, he didn't tell me I was a liar, and that alone was a miracle in my eyes. Finally, he said one thing. One wonderful thing.

'It's plausible.'

That was it, but the words brought hope with them.

He told me that I wouldn't be sent home, but the only place he had for me was a cell. He would leave the door open and I would have his personal assurance that I would be safe. CO Stewart said there would be a female officer outside all night and that he would look into the 'matter'.

I couldn't stop thanking him.

All he said was, again, 'It's plausible, Tracy – it is plausible.'

This was a man of fact, a man who liked proof and evidence. He could not accept all I was saying without uncovering more, but he was doing all he could to make me feel that I was being listened to and that he accepted this was something which could have happened. I did wonder whether he had ever heard anything about my dad, whether I was the final piece in the jigsaw, but he never gave anything away.

I was given an internal medical examination by an Army doctor at some point that night. I was so scared – and ashamed again – but the one thing that sticks in my mind is what I heard the doctor say to the nurse: *her hymen is broken.* His voice was low and serious, and although I didn't know what the word was, it seemed important. It wasn't until years later when I studied biology that I realised just *how* important. It was evidence. It was proof. However, all I could wonder at that point was, did the doctor mean that Dad had broken me? He had done so many things to my fragile little body, abused me in so many ways for so long, that it wouldn't have been a surprise if something was seriously wrong, so that word *broken* kept going round and round in my head.

The next day, when I was taken by the female officer who had stood watch outside my cell door to CO Stewart again, I was horrified to see my parents sitting outside his office door. While Dad stared at me with hatred on his face, Mum chose to make no eye contact with me at all. She never looked in my direction once, nor did she ask how I was or what was going on. I think that was when I finally realised that she must have known all along – her actions weren't the actions of a woman confused by her child's allegations against the man she loved, they were the actions of someone who didn't want to look in the face of the child she had betrayed, someone who was, no doubt, only concerned about what others would think.

I went into the Commanding Officer's room alone and he was just as kind as he had been when we first met. However, given a lifetime of disappointment, I was waiting for him to say that he didn't believe me and that Mum and Dad were there to drag me home.

Instead, he told me that I had two choices – one, to go with them, or two, to never go back again.

I couldn't believe it – really? *Really?* Was this wonderful man truly saying that it was entirely up to me and that I could, if I wanted, never, ever, ever go back to that place again?

I waited for the catch – but there was none.

The Army would pay for me to go to boarding school until I was sixteen. I now know what a huge deal this was. They must have been so sure of my father's guilt that they were moving heaven and earth to get me to a place of safety. All I had to do was go home for my things; if Dad was there, I wouldn't be alone with him, there would be an officer with me the whole time. In fact, if I chose, I would never have to be alone with him again for the rest of my life. I thanked CO Stewart profusely and left.

Mum chose not to be there when I went back to pack, her selfishness again leaving me vulnerable, but I collected my things as quickly as possible, stunned that Dad just accepted it, and amazed at the power CO Stewart must have wielded. I did wonder what he had threatened him with – Dad must have seen his hero status slipping away and it must have terrorised him into acquiescence.

Five minutes after I walked into that house, I walked out.

Those words are so powerful to me even to this day.

I walked out – that was it.

I went back to Army HQ ready to start my new life the next day, all because one man had finally listened, finally asked the right questions.

When morning dawned, I was happy but worried. I fully expected Dad to be there, laughing in my face and asking how I could have been so stupid as to believe this might happen. Even when I walked into the boarding school and met Matron, when I was given my uniform and introduced to the other girls, it all seemed surreal. Was this really the life I was allowed to have now?

I settled in surprisingly quickly. There were seven houses with over a hundred girls in each, and a boys' school five minutes away with the same set-up. All my classmates were from Army families, and all there for different reasons. I soon found out that some of them were there for the same reason as me. There were attempts at boarding school to maintain some sort of normal life and the staff tried to keep up appearances, and family visits were part of that. If mums and dads, and sometimes the siblings who hadn't been sent away, did turn up, it would generally be at weekends. It was more unusual for just one parent to turn up, and we tended to notice if that happened – in fact, we noticed everything. I think those of us with damaged pasts or broken families watched each interaction between children and parents like hawks, just to pick up any signs and, also, to see how other people acted.

One day, the little gang I had become part of sat in one of our usual haunts. There was a mini army assault course, which was situated just behind the house we lived in, and close to the fence that surrounded the school. It was used for girls and boys during PE lessons. There were rope ladders, nets to crawl under, horses to vault over, tyre swings and a climbing wall. Beside that assault course there was a tree, and we often gathered there when we wanted to smoke, especially if it was close to mealtime and we couldn't go far.

One of the girls in the group, Carly, was about fourteen years old and usually got visits from both parents. I can't remember what rank her father was but I do know that it wasn't anything high, such as a captain. I say this because all kids from high-ranking dads tended to stick together; the lower the rank the more likely it was for you to be an 'outsider'. Carly wasn't in with the 'snobby crowd' so it was likely that her dad had quite a low-level position.

As we were all hanging around smokers' tree, Carly said that her dad was coming that Saturday, a few days away.

'Is your mum coming too?' asked one of the other girls, Louise.

Carly laughed and said, 'No, so I guess I'll have to wear my navy knickers.'

165

'Why on earth would you have to do that?' asked Louise.

'Because he's weird, that's why,' replied Carly, 'but at least I'll get more pocket money from him if I do.'

None of us said anything, hoping that Louise would be the one to ask more questions about something that was clearly a bit odd, to say the least. She did.

'So you wear your navy knickers and you get more pocket money from him?'

'Not just my knickers but my whole gym kit too,' Carly went on. She thought for a few minutes, probably wondering whether to tell us any more. 'Sometimes I can get a record out of him as well as the cash.'

Sitting there, in a safe environment, I felt that I could ask questions, but I wasn't quite sure how to get to the heart of what Carly was saying. It wasn't right, and I wanted to know more. I wanted to know if her dad was like my dad.

'We're not allowed to be seen out with our gym kit on,' I said, joining in, but focusing on the rules. 'It's just for school.'

'I know that!' Carly snapped. 'I take it in my bag and put it on later when we get to the café, then change before we come back.'

'So you just sit in your kit?' asked Louise.

'Yeah,' replied Carly, 'he likes to look at me. Sometimes he takes me to the park. I go on the swings and he watches me in my knickers; he stands in front of me and pushes me higher so that he can look up my skirt.'

She shrugged as if there was nothing else to say about this, but Louise wasn't finished asking for more details.

'What does your mum say?' she enquired.

'About what?'

'About all *that*,' said Louise. 'About your dad wanting you to wear your gym kit and looking at your skirt and up your knickers and everything.'

'Well,' replied Carly, 'she doesn't know, obviously. Dad said he would stop taking me out and giving me money if I told her.'

I thought about this for a moment.

'Is your mum ill?' I asked Carly.

'No,' she answered. 'Why would she be? Why would you ask that?'

'Oh, I don't know,' I said, hoping no one else would dig too deep. 'Just asking.'

'I know what her dad is, though,' said Louise. 'He's a fucking whacko!'

Just then another girl came running up and asked if we knew that another girl had dumped her boyfriend. Our conversation stopped, as this seemingly vital piece of news was absorbed by Louise and Carly. It changed so quickly and moved into 'normal' teenage girl things, but I had a lot of questions I so wanted to ask Carly.

Does he touch you?

Do you touch him?

Are you his good girl?

I guess even if we hadn't been interrupted I would have been too scared to ask her these things – I still thought that other people would see me as disgusting if they found out what Dad had done to me, even though when I heard someone like Carly reveal that she too had an unnatural relationship with her father, I didn't think the same thing about her. *She* didn't seem disgusting; it was just me. I made sure to keep a lookout for her when she returned to school from her next trip out with her dad; she was laden with goodies and extra cash which she showed me as she also took her gym kit out of her bag.

Winking at me, she said, 'See? He's good for something at least.'

The lives and home situations of the other girls intrigued me, but I never drew attention to myself by asking too many questions or by being the one to initiate interrogations. There is obviously a natural nosiness in teenage girls, but I made sure that I only threw in a few questions if someone else started it off. The last thing I wanted was to become the focus of such questioning myself, but I did want to know whether they had good mums, good dads, good families. I clung on to tales of 'normality' just as I clung on to tales of families who seemed to be as disconnected and abusive as my own.

Carly ended up getting expelled about a year after revealing details about her dad. It was rumoured that she had been expelled because she had fallen pregnant by one of the boys from the school next to us. As always, the staff wouldn't reveal any details and no one seemed to ask any questions about why she would behave that way, but Carly did have a friend who she confided in at the school, Patricia, who couldn't wait to confirm the rumour for everyone once her 'friend' had gone. Patricia said that Carly's only response to her expulsion was, 'Great – at least it gets me away from Dad and from him being able to get me when he comes here.' Carly had told Patricia that her dad was 'giving her one' but as soon as she started having sex with other boys her father left her alone. I believed what Patricia said because to me it all seemed plausible (a word I liked very much since CO Stewart had used it).

Some of the girls confided in by Carly were the ones there when she told us about her dad and the gym kit. Someone asked Patricia if he was 'shafting her' then. The friend wasn't sure (I don't think she wanted to believe such things could even happen) and thought maybe he had tried but that Carly had exaggerated things just to get attention. We commented that where there was smoke there was fire – we thought we were really intelligent and knew every-thing about life! The strange thing was that among the group of girls she was telling we were not overly surprised about anything to do with sexual abuse. Had we all been faced with this? Was 'being good to Dad' a common thing? For other girls – the 'snobby' lot who were not really our friends – Carly soon became known as the tart of the house, and others spoke so cruelly about her that it again deterred me from speaking out fully.

I spent almost four years there, and I had many happy times. I was, truth be told, glad to be in such a structured place. I knew myself that I was in a better place, safe and not in a position to be abused again by Dad, as well as safe from Gary who would, I have no doubt, have turned out just like Dad. I don't doubt this because the truth was,

Gary had already tried to attack me. One day – not long after we had returned from our summer staying with family in Scotland while Mum was hospitalised – Gary and I were alone in the house, when he came into my room and sat on my bed. He said that he knew what I'd been doing and, when I pressed him on what he meant, he just kept saying that he knew, he knew. I didn't know what to think – did he actually mean that he knew Dad abused me? Was someone finally going to acknowledge what had been going on for so many years? Suddenly, Gary grabbed me, pulled me onto the bed, punched me in the stomach and tried to climb on top of me. His body was responding in just the same way as Dad and when I heard him start to grunt, breathing heavily as he got more and more excited, I found enough strength to get him off me, scratching and kicking like a mad thing. There was no way I was going to allow this to happen as well, I thought, no way I was going to let father *and* son abuse me. We never spoke of it after that day, but I never let my guard down around him again.

More importantly, though, as the years passed at boarding school, it was as if the ties had been severed from Mum. I really never had her in my life but, during my time there, I knew that I had to learn to do without her. I knew, deep down, that she would never come to see me, with or without Dad. I never got any presents from home, I never went back for Christmas. There were no visits, there was not even a pretence at maintaining any semblance of normal family life – at sixteen, I had to face up to the fact that I had absolutely no relationship with my mother, no relationship at all with the woman I had tried to save and protect since I was five years old.

Did it worry me? No: I had resolved myself to accept my situation and whatever life threw at me. As she had said, I was 'only' her daughter.

Did I want to see her again? No: I felt that she, as a mother, had let me down, turned her back on me and left me to my fate.

Was I angry? No, not in the least: anger came later, in adulthood. I was just glad to be where I was, apprehensive but safe.

Safer than I had ever dreamed I could be.

CHAPTER 10

FAIRY TALES

During my last year at boarding school, I had to make some decisions about what I would do when I left. I was actually not going to be quite sixteen when that school year finished, so I needed a legal guardian. Of course, I couldn't go home, having had virtually no contact with my parents since I was sent there, and the lack of prosecution regarding my father meant that it was still completely unsafe for me to be in his presence. I was desperate to get to the next stage in my life; legal freedom meant a great deal to me.

The head teacher, Miss Thorne, called me into her office one day, as she did with all the girls once they reached the point where they were about to leave school.

'Tracy,' she began, 'it has, generally . . .' and with that, she smiled, 'been a pleasure to have you here. Now that your time with us is coming to an end, however, I have certain responsibilities which I must ensure are carried out. Before you leave, there will be one more meeting with

173

me to formalise matters and to look at where you will go next.'

I knew all of that, but felt that there was more to come.

'Tracy — at that final meeting, legally, your father will have to be present,' she said. 'I'm afraid it's something that can't be got round, but I can give you my assurance that I will be with you at all times during that meeting.'

Over the next few days, I couldn't stop thinking about it. Everything at school was winding down; there was that strange air of happiness mixed with fear about what was happening to us all. The wide world was waiting for us and we were standing on the divide between childhood and adult life. In many ways, I was dreading leaving school. I had been safe there and I had known security, but I also desperately wanted the next part of my story to begin. All I had to do was get through seeing Dad again.

When the day came, I was filled with nerves, but I just kept telling myself that Miss Thorne would be there and that this was just one more hurdle to overcome — I'd been through worse. As soon as I walked into the office of the headmistress, she began speaking, almost as if she wanted to spare me the ordeal too and get it over as quickly as possible.

'Tracy has done very well,' she said, looking at me and smiling her encouragement the whole time. 'She is a really popular girl who has made lots of friends . . .'

I could only hear the words as background noise for I couldn't stop myself from reflecting on the changes that had occurred since I'd left home. I was older, taller, wiser, whereas Dad was heading into old age very quickly, even although he was only in his forties. He seemed worn down, pathetic, *nothing*. I found it hard to believe that he had held such power over me; he seemed so insignificant.

He just sat there, saying nothing, and I was quiet too with my own thoughts racing through my head. I heard Miss Thorne ask him a question.

'Could you please outline your plans for Tracy's future?' she demanded, in a strong voice.

Dad muttered something unintelligible.

'Can you please repeat that Mr Black? I need to know what Tracy will be doing next.'

Dad sighed and seemed completely uninterested.

'She's got family,' he said.

'Yes, I'm aware of that,' smiled Miss Thorne. 'But what are the plans of her family for her future?'

'She can go to them,' mumbled my father.

'Go where?'

'Away from here,' he replied.

'Scotland!' I jumped in. 'I want to go to Scotland.'

'Fine,' was his only reply, then he stood up and left the room without looking at me.

Miss Thorne looked embarrassed at this complete lack of parental interest but I could only think of my freedom. She was very nice to me – cut from the same cloth as CO Stewart, I always thought – and I prepared for my own passing-out day.

'You will have to be released into your father's care when your last day arrives, Tracy,' said Miss Thorne, She looked a little upset, but, to be honest, I had no fear of him any more. After seeing him at the last meeting, a broken old man, I knew that I was well out of his clutches and he would never draw me in again.

When Dad came to collect me, he said nothing in front of Miss Thorne, but as soon as we drove out of the school gates, that all changed.

'You . . .' he hissed. 'You're an evil little fucker, do you know that? I bet you do – I bet you love all of this attention. You've ruined my fucking life, you have.'

I stared ahead, telling myself that I just needed to get through this. He was taking me to the airport and, within hours, I'd be in Scotland, ready to start my new life away from him and away from his twisted view of what had happened.

'Your mum hates you,' he went on. 'Hates your fucking guts.'

I let out a bitter laugh at the irony of that remark. After all I had done 'for' her, I was now being told that she had chosen him, that she despised me.

He called me names all the way to the airport and I did my best to block him out by continuing to concentrate on flying away from him. As he drew up in a drop-off space, I jumped out of the car, grabbed my bag and slammed the door . He drove off without a word or a backwards glance. As the plane soared, I felt an enormous weight lift from me, but his words about Mum had cut me deeply.

When I got to Scotland, I moved in with some family members, Uncle Bobby – Dad's brother – and his wife

Wilma. They were nice enough people, although Wilma could be a bit stuck-up, and they never really questioned me about anything, which was a relief. They lived in a little village on the east coast, within commuting distance of Edinburgh, and had a quiet life. I think they just believed I was going through a teenage phase of wanting my own life and that was the reason I had left Germany. Wilma did often talk about my 'posh' boarding school education and wonder why I wasn't going to university, but she tended to wonder aloud rather than ask me direct questions, so I could avoid the whole business. I wasn't allowed to stay on my own until I was sixteen, and there were three weeks between leaving school and my birthday, so I worked on a local farm, 'howking tatties' (pulling potatoes up) and cleaning the chicken coops. I was counting the minutes until I was legally responsible for myself, and also applying elsewhere for other jobs.

Wilma was very concerned about money and she was keen for me to get something better paid than farm work, so I could contribute more to the household fund. After three weeks she'd had her fill of me, and although she was never nasty, it was obvious that I needed to either make the situation financially attractive to her, or get out. I managed to get a job in a big hotel in Edinburgh and travelled in there each day for a little while, but Wilma complained that I was spending too much on buses which was, in effect, money she was losing out on. The only solution I could see was to move out, which is what I did. I was allowed to stay in a tiny little box room in the hotel for free. It might not have been much for a lot of people, but it represented freedom to me. I had no one telling me what to do when I closed the door after my shift as a waitress ended. I was away from Germany and away from my parents. Everything else would come in time, of that I was sure.

I often said to myself that I enjoyed my own company and I enjoyed my freedom, but actually, I'm not sure whether that was entirely accurate or whether I was just trying to convince myself, because one thing I did notice during this period of my life was that I seemed to have a complete inability to make friends. When I stayed with my aunt and uncle, I stayed away from the other workers through choice. They were all much older than me, most of them in their thirties, and I would just get on with my work and then go back to the house, where I would stay indoors as much as I could. I never ventured far.

Dad had always kept me away from others and, as a child, I had never really developed positive interaction skills. Combined with this, Mum had ridiculed me and made me feel so inferior that when I was free from her, I was afraid others would see me that way too. I wondered whether I would ever shed that feeling that she was telling the truth after all – that I was a bother to everyone, that I was stupid, that I deserved bad things. Despite the fact that I had escaped, and had actually been away from Mum for some time now, she was still having a huge effect on me.

When I met people for the first time, I always wondered if I could trust them, especially men – I would look out for the same mannerisms in them that Dad always displayed;

for example, he would lick his moustache and then wipe it with his thumb and index finger, or sometimes he would shake his handkerchief before using it. If I saw any man doing these things, it would make me break out in a sweat and become very flustered and scared. I also had many recurrent nightmares, often after seeing another man display these mannerisms. I would wake up with the night terrors and lie awake until morning, unable to stop the replay of my childhood in my head.

There was only one problem at the hotel where I worked – as a new girl there, and as a young one with no family around her, I was seen, pretty much, as fresh meat. I hated the attention and hated how I always felt I was there just as a 'thing' for men. There were so many men there, staff as well as guests, and I was pawed about from the start. One man, Trevor, was a cocksure kind of guy who was always flirting with the girls, especially the new ones like me. He said that I was a challenge because of my accent, but I didn't really have one so I always suspected that was just a line. Although I was, technically, Scottish, the bases and moving around had rubbed the edges away so I just had a very generic sort of twang, nothing that could really identify me geographically. Army brats have a mixture of all accents that tend to cancel each other out, but I think Trevor found it odd that he couldn't quite place me or my background from how I spoke.

I rebuffed all of his advances as I really wasn't interested in the slightest. The other hotel workers thought it was because I had a 'tip' about myself, that I felt I was better than everyone else, especially when it came out that I had been to boarding school. Not knowing my real background, and being given no information by me, they all decided that I was a snob, which was a long way from the truth. I was happy for them to think this way, though, as I wanted no one to know what my story really was. It all made Trevor adamant that he was going to get a date with the 'posh girl'.

He was head butler while I was a waitress, so we saw a lot of each other on our shifts, but I tried to avoid him as much as possible. Trevor was good-looking, not too tall but very sure of himself. He had dark blond hair and sallow skin, much more handsome than his brother, Dan, who also worked at the hotel. But Dan was in fact the only one who didn't try it on and who didn't make me feel uncomfortable. He was a bit of an oddball himself, always dressed in a black-collared green Crombie coat, with great big glasses. He definitely was different to other men and I felt safe around. I wanted someone quiet and reserved, not someone like Trevor, who was far too assertive and worldly for me. And that's what I thought I'd found in Dan. I was seeking a quiet, subdued life – with Trevor it would have been all nightclubbing and parties, an alien world for me and one I didn't want. Once or twice I even threw crockery at him and screamed that he needed to leave me alone, but this only made him more determined, and resulted in him telling everyone that he loved a 'feisty one'. I actually think that the other guys must have had a bet on as to whether he would get a date with me or not. Trevor persevered for a while until I finally told him in no uncertain terms to get lost and leave me alone. I didn't actually realise that he was Dan's brother until quite a while later, after I went out with Dan, as they were like chalk and cheese, so different in every way. I thought that it was similar to the relationship between me and Gary. We may have been from the same family, but everything about us was opposite, just like Dan and Trevor.

While Trevor relied on his looks to catch a girl's eye, Dan was much more subtle. He had a great sense of humour, was three years older than me, and didn't seem to care that he looked absolutely ridiculous in the clothes he wore. We went out for a drink a few times and got on really well. Despite what I had been through, I was quite naive. I didn't have normal experiences, a normal background, and my whole view of relationships was totally twisted. I loved that Dan made me laugh. I started to think that he was the sort who would stay, the sort you could trust. I thought he was so different from any other man I'd ever known. It was too soon, of course it was – I had only left school a few months earlier and I'd never had a real boyfriend, but the inevitable happened: we kissed and I was head over heels with him before I knew what was happening.

As things developed with Dan, I began to wonder whether it might be a good idea to move out of the hotel. I had lost count of the advances made to me by other men when I had first started – it's not that I considered myself irresistible, but just another indication to me of how men (and perhaps many women) seemed to see me as fair game. Even though my accommodation was free and I had no travelling costs, I began to worry that they all knew I stayed there and I dreaded someone knocking on my door late at night, trying their luck, so I began to ask around to find out if someone knew of any cheap, local digs.

Dan mentioned to me that his auntie had a spare room and that she was looking for a new lodger. I jumped at the chance. I admit that I was already getting very clingy, I wanted to be with Dan all the time and I saw this as an opportunity to be even closer. Everything that had gone on in Germany and Northern Ireland was still there, it would never disappear, but I was desperate to make a new life – to make a new me. Dan was to be part of that, in my eyes. I loved the fact that we worked together and that he was my boyfriend, and I now felt that, if we had an opportunity to be linked through his auntie, we'd have an even higher chance of staying together.

I met Auntie Gloria as soon as possible, nervously think-ing of what I could do or say to impress her. I shouldn't have worried, she was only interested in getting another lodger as quickly as possible and making sure that the rent money was paid on time as she had her own life, and a busy job.

'Are you working?' she asked, even though she must have known through Dan that I was.

I nodded.

'Do you get to keep all your money or does your mum take it?'

'I get to keep it,' I answered. 'Mum doesn't – well, my parents live abroad. I don't have anything to do with them.'

'You a hard worker?'

I nodded.

'Clean? Tidy?'

I nodded again.

'You don't say much, do you?' she smiled. 'That's fine by me – pay your rent on time, don't cause a fuss, that's all I need. Move in when you like, love.'

With that, she left the room and I wondered why I had been so worried. Gloria was certainly no-nonsense, but she was also a kind woman and one I would become very fond of. I soon came to understand that if she was brusque, it was only because she was always busy. I quickly got all my things together; I had very little, only enough clothes to fill a bag and a few other bits and pieces, but I felt terribly grown-up and terribly free. The room was in a flat in Leith, an area to the north of Edinburgh, busy and noisy, poor and dirty. The whole place has undergone a superficial transformation in recent years, with affluent types trying to turn it into a gentrified offshoot of the capital, but the changes only go skin deep – there are many parts of Leith that are no different to when I lived there all those years ago. I didn't care what it looked like. I was closer than ever to Dan. He seemed to be happy with me too, and I tagged along whenever he met his friends. I still had none of my own, so our worlds were completely intertwined. Looking back, I know that I was too dependent on him, too quickly, but it was all happening in a glow of first love and I saw no harm in it.

Dan's parents had separated a while before I met him, and I had got the impression from Dan and Trevor that their mother doted on them. I was excited to meet Cathy, Dan's mum, as I hoped I would take to her as quickly as I had taken to Gloria, but she turned out to be a million miles away from the sort of woman I had imagined. I think, subconsciously, I had wondered if Cathy could be the kind of mother I'd never had myself, but in reality she was an interfering busybody, an alcoholic shambles of a woman who was only happy if she had a bottle in her hand and her nose in someone else's business. Her drinking and her attitude soon crushed any fantasies I might have entertained about forming a bond with her.

On the night we went to visit Cathy for the first time, Dan knocked and knocked at the door, but there was no answer. He finally let himself in with a key that was left under the mat. There was a woman sprawled out on the sofa, blind drunk and lying in her own vomit. She was surrounded by empty bottles and smelled like nothing I'd ever been around before.

I stood there open-mouthed as Dan tried to shake her into consciousness. It didn't work.

'Is she all right?' I asked. 'Do we need to call an ambulance?'

'What for?' he asked, looking genuinely confused.

'For your mum,' I whispered, pointing towards the heap in front of us.

'That's not my mum,' he said. 'It's . . . one of my aunties.'

184

With that blatant lie, he took my hand and led me out of the house, back to Gloria's flat.

Later that night, I raised it again.

'Do you think your mum's fine?' I wondered aloud.

There was a pause.

'Do you mean because she wasn't there when we went to visit?' asked Dan. 'Do you mean because my auntie was there and Mum wasn't?'

This was mad, I thought to myself. We both knew that was his mum, not some unnamed auntie, but if he wanted to maintain a fiction, who was I to burst it all open, given what I was hiding? I said no more, and a few days later we went back to meet Cathy for the 'first' time. It was as if nothing had ever happened. What I did find out about the sober, conscious Cathy was that no one would ever have been good enough for her son – for either of her sons – but I was very far down her list of what she expected from a prospective daughter-in-law. As Dan and I spent more and more time together, she had to face up to the fact that I was exactly that: the woman her eldest son would marry – and she hated it.

By the time I was seventeen, my life had changed completely. I was still working at the hotel, living in Gloria's flat, and in a relationship with Dan – but I was also getting ready for the next stage of my life. Everything had progressed, including the sexual side of things. Despite the fact that I'd been exposed to sexual experiences since I was a very young child, the first time I slept with Dan terrified me – it was a completely different experience, as it should be. What had happened with my father had not been based on consent; it had been a nasty, twisted exploitation of a child by the man who should have protected her. When he raped me, it may have been sexual for him, but it was also about power and control. Until Dan, I had never had a sexual relationship based on equality and willingness. I loved him and I wanted to show him that love in every way I could, but it was still terrifying for me. Anything to do with sex had always been negative and manipulative in my life, and I tried with all my heart to turn that round. I wouldn't say it was perfect, but at least I wanted it to happen. I tried to convince myself that I was normal now, that I had moved on from my past, but there were always ghosts. Every time Dan touched me, I had to push away thoughts of other things. Every time I felt something nice, I had to ignore the fact that I had been touched before. Every time I recognised my own sexual feelings, I heard a voice telling me that I was a dirty little whore. It was all so complicated and difficult, every little bit of happiness I managed to secure for myself was hard-fought.

Dan would often asked me why I had never had a boyfriend before. I used the excuse of the all-girls boarding school but I don't think it really convinced him at all. He even suggested at one time that maybe I was into girls, and I wondered whether he actually believed that or whether he was relying on some pathetic, male cliché of what boarding schools were. He did ask me why I was always so keen to bathe after we had sex, but I just told him that I thought every girl washed after sex. I knew that he wasn't a virgin when I met him, but he would emphasise this by saying that none of his other girlfriends had ever done it. He questioned whether I thought he was dirty and that's why I always rushed to wash afterwards, but I just reassured him that it meant nothing.

I hadn't told Dan of my past, not the detail of it, but his mother was like a dog with a bone. She was always niggling at me, always asking questions. *Where did you say your parents lived now? Where did you say your auntie and uncle were? Why did they send you away to boarding school? Where's your brother? Do you have an address for your parents? Maybe I should write to them, introduce myself, one big happy family?*

I avoided her questions whenever I could, but she never let up. When avoiding the topic didn't work, I lied, but I always worried that I wouldn't be able to keep track of the stories I told her. I just wanted her to stop questioning me and asked Dan if he could get her to back off; but he never saw anything but good in his mother, and told me to stop being so paranoid.

The truth was that she was a dreadful woman. She seemed to resent me staying with Gloria, even more so now that Dan had moved in too, and the worst arguments came while we lived there. I think Cathy felt that if Gloria hadn't put a roof over my head, I would have moved on and Dan could have found another girlfriend. All of the arguments were the same. She insulted me constantly, saying that I wasn't good enough for her son, that I was a little tart, that I thought I was better than anyone else – and every comment was littered with swearing.

'He'll fucking dump you soon enough, you little fucking tart,' she'd scream at me every time I saw her.

Sometimes, going out to get some shopping or heading back to the flat, Cathy would spot me from inside one of the many bars nearby and come running out, screaming.

'I'm fucking going to tell fucking Dan that you were with a fucking other bloke you fucking dirty fucking tart!' She could barely speak without swearing, sometimes even splitting words up by putting 'fucking' in the middle. I would ignore her and she would turn to other people walking by and say, 'See that fucking tart there? Fucking whore, that is!'

If I'd had a choice, I would have stayed well away from her, but, friendless and still unsure of myself, I continued to hope for a real-life fairy tale. All I had was Dan, the only people I met were his friends and Cathy's friends. He spent a lot of time with his mother, so, by default, I did too. If he wanted to visit her, I went too, because I wanted to be with him all the time. He was a real mummy's boy and everything Cathy said meant more to him than anything, but still he felt like the one for me, the one for life.

For a while, everything was fine – not perfect, but I only had imperfect things to compare life with anyway. I kept my own money for the first year or so of our relationship but then we both lost our jobs at the hotel when it closed for refurbishment. I picked up work again quickly, I was never scared of hard graft, but Dan saw it as an opportunity to laze around and do nothing. The arguments began and, in my heart of hearts, I knew that this wasn't how things should be. But I still held on to the good times and thought that, if I did everything right, they might turn into the 'always' times. Dan was a charmer. When we were talking, he would promise me the world – a nice house with a garden, a car, plenty of kids who would never want for anything. All the usual promises men like him always make and always will. He said he would get a job, a good one, and I'd never go short; but actually, he never worked again, not at anything legal, and he was always very reluctant to give me any money he did make.

In that first year, I knew things were changing but I was always very soft where Dan was concerned. Our relationship was far from perfect – like his mother, Dan liked to shout, and I bore the brunt of his verbal anger. We had moved out of Gloria's by this point, into our own little house, and so I had no one to turn to, no one to protect me when he would go off on one of his rants. I told myself that it was hard for him not to have the job and the lifestyle he thought he should have, but I never faced up to the obvious – he was his own worst enemy. We argued a lot about his mother and how much she tried to interfere, and I did give as good as I got.

'She's a nasty old bitch!' I shouted one day. 'She won't be happy till she's split us up, and I don't want that, I don't want her to ruin our relationship because we could be so good together, Dan.'

He lunged towards me and shoved me as hard as he could, pushing me into the wall before he banged his way out of the house. I felt sorry for him. His mother was nasty and I knew all about nasty mums, so I didn't really blame him for how he reacted. I was so naive. When I finally did realise that he wasn't even trying to find a respectable job, the arguments escalated – and so did the violence.

'Are you ever going to get a proper job?' I asked him one day, after we had, yet again, argued about his mother sticking her nose into things.

'Are you ever going to shut the fuck up?' he retorted.

'I'll shut up when you bring some steady money in,' I replied. It was like that a lot of the time. He was getting lazier and lazier, I was finding it hard to keep everything going on my wage, I would say something, he would get angry. It was a recipe for disaster; but, this time, he didn't react – not verbally.

'Did you hear me?' I said. 'We need steady money – that's all it takes, Dan. We can plan our lives when you get a job, we can move on.'

Before I knew what was happening, he had hit me so hard that the chair I was sitting in was knocked back, with me on it. I lay on the floor, dazed and confused.

'Tracy!' Dan said, standing over me. 'Oh my God, Tracy – are you all right, my darling?'

I just looked at him – had he really hit me? Had he really hit me *that* hard?

'I'm so sorry, I'm so sorry, Tracy,' he wailed. 'I wasn't thinking – you were just going on and on, winding me up, and I just snapped. I'll never, *never* do that again. I'll never hurt you, I promise with all my heart.' He was cradling me in his arms as he said all of this and the tears started to flow from his eyes. 'I hate myself, I really do – how could I do that to you? By God, it'll be the last time, I can promise you that.'

He lied.

Of course he lied.

Throwing me across the room, whacking me on the head, slapping me, punching me – it became a way of life. All the time, I tried to convince myself he'd never been taught right from wrong. He would make all sorts of promises, say he would change, blame his mum, and I desperately wanted to believe him.

I had become very close to Auntie Gloria by this point. She was a caring woman, although not in an overly emotional way. She was sensible and pragmatic, willing to help anyone who was down on their luck, but she didn't suffer fools gladly. She'd had plenty of run-ins with her sister, and warned me off Cathy many times.

'She'll take and take but you'll get nothing back,' said Gloria. 'All she cares about is herself and her boys. You watch yourself, lass, you mind your own back.'

Gloria never pried or attempted to find out anything about my past – would I have confided in her? I'm not sure. There were times when I wanted to scream from the memories that rushed back into my head and I often did feel that I wanted to offload onto someone else, but there was always the fear that, if I did, they would change their opinion of me. I thought a lot of Gloria, and I would have hated it if she had started to see me as the dirty little whore who had lured her own father into a sexual relationship, because that was exactly the type of thing I did tell myself when things got bad. All of the insults and hate from my parents over the years turned into cold, hard facts and I held on to the one truth in my life – I had Dan, and I had to keep his love. Not revealing my past to him or his mother was something I could do, but I did sometimes wish I could tell Gloria. Writing this now, I think she would have been a good person to share things with. I wish I had trusted myself to confide in her.

About six months after Dan and I lost our jobs at the hotel, when I was still just seventeen, he took me out for a meal one night. He knew I was becoming very upset by Cathy's constant interrogations and I thought he was going to tell me that I needed to just stop being bothered, or try a bit harder with her.

I settled into my seat at the cheap Italian restaurant and looked at the all-you-can-eat buffet around us. It was hardly the height of sophistication but, as always, the fact that I was there, alone with Dan, was all that mattered to me. He seemed quite nervous which, in turn, made me wary and I couldn't help but wonder whether something his mum had said to him had stuck. She was always dripping poison into his ear and I knew that, while no other woman would be perfect for him in her eyes, I was a long way from even being acceptable. When she was in one of her foul-mouthed drunken rants, Cathy would call me names that reminded me of those my father used to say. It completely threw me – although she was only (only!) being insulting and obnoxious, a chill would still run through me when she said I was a 'whore' or a 'slut', that I was 'no good' or 'man mad'. Deep down, I knew she would have said those things to anyone who dared to take her boy away (as she saw it), but she had no idea how deep they really cut me. We all carry our childhoods with us, and an abused child shoulders those dark times forever.

As I sat there, I wondered whether Cathy had finally persuaded Dan that she was right, that he should leave me, that I wasn't worthy of his love. It took a while for what he was really saying to register.

'Tracy? Tracy?' he said, over and over again, and the words finally penetrated.

'Sorry . . .' I muttered.

'Well, will you?' he asked.

'Erm, will I . . .?' I repeated, trying to work out what his previous question had been.

'Marry me! Please, Tracy – please will you be my wife?'

Marry him! Marry Dan! It was beyond my wildest dreams – as I'd sat there, worrying that he was going to say it was all over, he'd been getting stressed that I might turn him down!

I looked at him, sitting there, holding out a cheap, flimsy engagement ring – and it seemed the most beautiful thing in the world to me. It was a tiny gold ring, with a garnet in the middle and little cubic zirconia all around. I loved it. When I said 'yes', all our fights and worries disappeared from my mind. Dan said that getting married, being a real couple, would get us away from his mother. We would have a fresh start together and she couldn't complain that I was a gold-digger if we were husband and wife. The fact that she said this was ludicrous anyway. I worked as many hours as I could in two jobs, at a bingo hall and cleaning, while Dan usually wasted the day away on her sofa.

We both wanted to get married quickly, and that night, as we made our future plans, Dan promised to get a proper job as soon as possible; he said it would be something secure and respectable. I believed him, and just hoped it would be quick – I wanted a real house with a real family, and I needed him to pull his weight. The only 'work' he ever seemed to do was stripping lead off roofs, and collecting copper, both of which could get him into trouble with the police at any point. I could only earn so much in my jobs, but I fell for all his promises that night as he said he would make me proud and provide for us both.

He wanted to tell his mother immediately and, although I dreaded this, I went along with it. We walked back to her house but, of course, she was still at the pub. Dan let us in with his key and we held each other tightly as we waited for Cathy to be thrown out at closing time. I knew she'd go ballistic, but Dan tried to calm me down with soothing words and more promises. He was blind where his mother was concerned and there was only so much I was willing to say, as I knew a wedge could be driven between us if I pointed out just how awful she was. He had to see it for himself.

We heard her that night long before she crashed into the house. She was shouting obscenities in the street below and arguing with people out there while we waited with our good news. When Cathy finally staggered into the living room, she was close to passing out.

'My darling boy!' she yelled at Dan, launching herself at him. 'Oh, for fuck's sake – you've got that little bitch with you!' she continued as she saw me beside him.

'Now, that's enough of that, Mum,' said Dan, trying to keep the peace. 'I've got something to tell you.'

'Is it good news?' she asked, squinting her eyes at him.

'Aye, it is,' he replied.

'Then it can only mean one thing!' Cathy shouted. 'You're getting rid of that sour-faced whore! This calls for a drink!' She rolled out of the room, looking for vodka as Dan looked at me, aghast.

'I don't think we should tell her,' I said. 'I don't want her to know about the wedding – let's just make it about us,' I begged.

'Did you bring that bitch so that I could spit in her face one last time?' cackled Cathy from the kitchen. 'Good fucking riddance!' she went on.

As she continued to look for a drink – any drink – Dan whispered to me, 'You're right – let's go.' We crept out of the room and into the street. He held me in his arms as we both looked back at the window where his mother could be seen, dancing around on her own, a glass in her hand.

I vowed I would never be like that. I rarely drank anyway, but the thought of losing myself, of being out of control, horrified me. I would never become that sort of woman. Dan and I kissed, with the sounds of the busy city ringing in our ears. It felt as if we were the only people in the world. I knew I could change him; I knew I could make everything perfect. Dan would get a job – a good job – we would save and make our own little family. I would never have to see my parents again and we could cut Cathy out of our lives, because we would be strong together. The fights which had started to become a feature of our relationship would disappear once Dan got out of the clutches of that awful woman and found his own feet; he would be loving and gentle all the time, he would stop hitting me, stop the violence that was now part of my life with him. It would be like a fairy tale come true. I'd make it all so special.

I would.

I had to.

CHAPTER 11

WEDDED BLISS

We tried hard to keep news of the wedding away from Cathy, but, to be honest, I was never sure whether she knew or not. Leith was like a little village rather than part of a capital city – everyone knew everyone else, and they all liked nothing better than a good gossip. I really didn't think we'd be able to keep the wedding a secret from her, as other people would find out soon enough and start talking, but if we were going to try, the wedding itself would have to be soon. We went along to the Registrar's Office and were given a date about two months ahead. As we left, Dan squeezed my hand.

'You'll see,' he whispered. 'It'll all work out.'

I smiled, desperate to believe him, but sure that Cathy would stop it all if she could. It was a difficult time. After even more arguing, Dan finally agreed that he would try to bring in some steady money, but I felt that he was saying it to appease me rather than making any commitment. The easy-going nature I had loved in him was changing and starting to show itself as laziness and violence.

I clung on to the good things in my life – one of which was Gloria. We had become friends quickly and I now counted her among the very few people I would trust. She was such a nice woman, very private, but happy to sit and chat with me when we were alone together. She liked to talk about her job, about some of the eccentric people she came into contact with as part of it. We would have a good laugh about some of their antics and she would have me rolling about with laughter.

'One man asked me to marry him today,' she giggled, settling down at the kitchen table.

'Ooh, what did you do to deserve that?' I asked.

'Apparently I made the best cup of tea he had ever tasted,' Gloria replied. 'Good enough to make him propose!' We would often sit and have a natter at the end of the day, sharing stories until Dan came back, often to start a fight.

She knew Dan and I were arguing a lot but she would take my hand and pat it, while telling me to keep persevering and stay away from Cathy. If Dan was in as well and we had been arguing, Gloria would scowl at him and say, 'Don't you be turning out like your dad now.' Dan would apologise and say it was all over something stupid and wouldn't happen again, but it always did.

Gloria would tell me stories about her childhood, where she went to school, what the fashions were back then, and where she worked over the years. She had never married and she never had kids, but if I ever asked about that, she would just bow her head and shake it, then change the subject. On the whole, she just went about her daily business, which she loved, until one day she got sick and ended up being admitted to hospital with tuberculosis. I was terribly upset when she died just a few weeks before we were due to marry. She had never become a mother figure to me exactly, but she had also never done anything bad to me and had been very supportive when she could see that I was trying to get Dan to make something of himself.

The wedding was to take place in a registry office in Leith, next to Victoria Baths. It was a straightforward affair. I had found myself a pretty little white dress with turquoise flowers from Debenhams. From a second-hand shop, I got a matching pillbox hat and shoes, finishing off by buying some turquoise lace and making a small veil for the front of the hat. I also made the bouquet myself from artificial flowers and white ribbon. Dan hired a suit and looked as handsome as he ever would – even he admitted that wasn't much, but he did his best! It didn't matter to me; I just wanted to begin our fairy tale.

Our witnesses were Trevor and his latest girlfriend. Trevor managed to pull me aside and seemed incredulous that I would have chosen Dan over him – he hadn't changed since our days working in the hotel together. Dan's dad and stepmother were also there, but I barely knew them at that point. It was all very low key. We got married late in the afternoon and went straight to the pub afterwards for the reception. It wasn't far to go, but we piled into a taxi nonetheless as a special treat.

We knew the landlady, Maggie, well and she was delighted with our happy news. She made the very kind gesture of laying on a little buffet for us when our friends all turned up some time later. There were only about twenty people coming, but it was still a weight off our minds, as money was incredibly tight. Dan's dad had bought our wedding cake, so our only expenses on the day were the registrar and a photographer.

I still couldn't believe that Cathy had stayed away. When I saw the pub all decorated with streamers and balloons, flowers and ribbons, all courtesy of Maggie, I felt as if I would burst with happiness. It was lovely. Music was playing and our friends turned up, making sure that the celebration was small but warm. As I danced with Dan, I felt as if this was a fresh start and I would do all I could to be a good wife.

But after about two hours, my bubble was well and truly burst. Drunk as a skunk, Cathy rolled into the pub, shouting and swearing at everyone.

'Here they are!' she shrieked. 'Here's the little bitch who's taken my son away from me!'

Dan put his arm around my shoulders, protectively, and we waited for Cathy to run out of steam. Everyone kept their eyes down – they'd seen it all before from her.

'Keeping me away as if I'm not good enough for you,' she bawled, jabbing her finger in my face. 'You're the one who's not good enough for *him*!' she finished, pointing at Dan.

Dan said nothing, but his dad came over and tried to calm Cathy down. It didn't work – it never did with her

– and, before long, my wedding party had erupted into a fight, with Dan's parents laying into each other as all hell broke loose.

'I'm off – I can't stand this!' I told Dan, who was following me as I made my way out of the door in tears. 'I just can't bear it, Dan – I need to go or I'll scream.'

'Fair enough,' he said, and walked back inside.

I waited outside the pub for some time, thinking that he must just be saying goodbye to people and apologising for his mother's behaviour, but it finally dawned on me that he had chosen to stay there and mollify her rather than come with me on his wedding night. There was no way I would go back in there – I knew that Cathy would have headed straight for me, so, still weeping, I went to a friend's house. I was in bits. I couldn't believe that my wedding day had ended like this. After all I had been through, I had hoped this day was a sign that things were changing. I was Dan's wife and I wanted that to symbolise a new start. I had hoped it would make Cathy face up to the fact that nothing could tear us apart, that her son had chosen to marry me and that we were going to make a good life together – instead, on our first night as husband and wife, I was crying alone and he had gone back to drinking in the pub. It wasn't exactly the honeymoon I had planned for, but I wasn't surprised that Cathy had managed to ruin it. She was as obsessed with Dan as Mum had ever been with Gary.

The next morning, my friend woke me with all the news. She had a newborn baby, which was why she hadn't been able to come to the reception, and, as she jiggled the little boy up and down in her arms, she informed me that Cathy had been thrown out of the pub by Maggie after I had left, with a few home truths from the loyal landlady. Cathy had tried to get back in and the police had been called to eject her permanently.

I wondered why Dan hadn't found me then – he would have known which friend I was staying with. It transpired that the reception had continued for many hours and Dan had been paralytic by closing time.

He didn't turn up until late that afternoon.

'I'm so sorry, so sorry,' he began as soon as he was let into the flat. 'Mum was in a terrible state. How can I make it up to you?'

'She ruined everything, Dan,' I told him. 'How can you possibly make up for that?'

'I know, I know – but she doesn't know what she's doing when she's drunk,' he answered.

'But what about you? What about your part in it? You could have left with me, but you chose to take her side again – on our wedding day!'

'It was nothing to do with me,' he lied. 'I had to stay there, it was only polite – the groom couldn't piss off as well as the bride, after all!'

This was so typical of him. I kept pushing all the niggles out of my mind, trying to focus on how wonderful my life as a wife would be – but there was always a little voice saying *you'll never be happy, you don't deserve it.*

I had been feeling quite unwell in the weeks before the wedding. I was tired all the time and sick most days, but I had put it down to stress – especially given how difficult Dan's mother was being – and normal bride-to-be jitters. However, when I went back to work on the Monday after we married, I took a funny turn. I was working in a big bingo hall and, when I tried to pick up and move a huge tea urn, I passed out.

Given that I hadn't been feeling quite right, I thought I should go to the doctor – and was shocked when the first thing he suggested was a pregnancy test. I didn't tell Dan what had happened as I felt it very unlikely that I would be having a baby. I'd always wondered whether my dad's abuse had damaged me internally in some way, and the Army doctor's phrase about me being 'broken' still rang in my ears, so when Dan and I had started our physical relationship, it just hadn't occurred to me that we needed to use contraceptives.

When I went back for the results that Friday, I could hardly believe what I heard.

Positive.

Pregnant.

I was having a baby!

Eighteen and just married, the next stage of my life was to begin in earnest. I went home and told Dan immediately.

'Thank God you didn't find out before we got married!' he said.

'Why not?' I asked. 'What difference would it have made?'

'It would have given my mum something else to moan about,' he replied. 'She would have said it was the only reason we got hitched in the first place.'

I sat there waiting for a clue, some indication of what he felt about this life-changing news – I didn't know if he was pleased or not; his first thought had been for his mother, as usual. But then Dan punched the air with happiness and shouted, 'I'm going to be a dad!' I was delighted by his reaction, and by the words that followed. 'I'm a man now, Tracy – I've got to grow up, I've a family to look after.'

We sat together for a little while and he rubbed my tummy, then announced that he was off out to celebrate by getting drunk. The grown-up approach hadn't lasted long, but I couldn't begrudge him a night out as our lives were going to face a big upheaval. I felt the same way as my husband in that I wanted to be very adult about this and do everything properly. As I sat alone on the sofa, I vowed to the child in my belly that I would be a better mother than the one I had known. I would love it unconditionally and forever, protect it from harm, and never leave the little boy or girl to the mercy of others. I loved Dan, but I swore that I would never put him before my child and that if the new life inside me ever said anything to make me question things, I would believe them in a way I had never been believed.

It wasn't long before I became quite poorly with morning sickness, and this would continue for the whole pregnancy. Dan couldn't do enough for me to begin with, but after a while he got bored of it.

'Anything I can get you? Cup of tea? Cushion?' he would ask at the start, but it soon changed to, 'Christ, are you throwing up again? Get some fucking dignity, will you?'

He would be at his mum's house a lot of the time, and she always encouraged him to drink with her. I know that it made him more likely to listen to her poison about me.

'I can't wait to get my new baby!' she would say to me on the few occasions she visited. Cathy always made a point of emphasising that she saw my unborn child as *hers* and that she would be taking as much control as possible.

'I hope it's a boy,' she would say. 'Boys always love their mummies – I don't want a girl, they're too much bother.' Yes, she probably did think boys were a lot easier, as her own never seemed to question or challenge her.

Dan stayed out a lot, sometimes not coming back at night at all, and when he did, he was roaring drunk and verbally abusive.

'I'm sick of seeing you sitting there doing fuck all!' he'd snarl. 'Is this fucking pregnancy ever going to end? You're making a meal of it, aren't you?'

I felt awful. I had no real experience of pregnancy as I'd never had that normal extended family life with female relatives getting pregnant and passing new-borns around for cuddles; I hadn't realised that some women – like me – were so ill throughout. While I was determined to be the best mother I could be, I was shocked at how draining the physical side of being pregnant was and I felt very depend-ent on my totally unreliable husband.

I had no one really, other than the friend I'd stayed with on my wedding night – she was a comfort, but she was also busy coping with her new baby. I'd always found it hard to trust and this was a time that I would have loved to have a mother by my side, or a mother figure. My own mum wasn't an option, Gloria was dead, and Cathy hated me. I felt as if I was on my own and this, in itself, brought back memories of my childhood and the loneliness of that time. I was scared but I also knew that I'd been through worse and that I could cope by myself if I had to. Somehow, I did find strength, even when the doctors told me that I had a low-lying placenta and that the baby might be in danger. I was ill for nine months, but there was a great comfort to be found from telling myself that I would be better than my mum at this. It kept me going.

In the dark moments, though, there was one thought which bothered me, one niggle which kept returning. I started to question whether I would indeed love the baby the way I wanted to. What if love didn't come naturally? I clung on to the thought that, because I wanted this baby so much, there was no chance that I wouldn't love it. I believed that Mum had actively chosen *not* to love me, and I vowed never to fall into that trap. My baby would be my world.

I bought most of my maternity clothes from charity shops (a habit I still have to this day). I was very thin so didn't need a lot, in fact, I was being sick so much that I barely weighed seven stones. The fashion back then was for long denim skirts or jeans, and big, floppy jumpers, all of which did as well when I was pregnant as when I wasn't. I got a few things from those places for the baby too, but I wanted him or her to have lovely new clothes so, against the odds, I taught myself to knit. I spent hours making cardigans and coats, even shawls. Dan's dad and stepmother were very good to us too, buying lots of gifts throughout the whole pregnancy for the grandchild who was coming, including a big Silver Cross pram.

Dan's attitude was confusing. On the one hand, he was so proud that I was pregnant and told everyone he met, but I soon realised this was a very basic thing and actually reflected that he felt he had proven himself as a man, rather than showing any love for me and our family. Perhaps he felt threatened that he would no longer have all my attention, or perhaps he hated the thought that he was bound forever to the woman who his adored mother despised, I don't know, but as my pregnancy progressed, his violence towards me escalated. I was always looking for excuses for him and put the increasing violence down to us finding our way with each other, having a baby, the lack of money, and the stress from all of it. The only money he brought in was from thieving, but he barely gave me a pittance.

'Have you managed to earn anything this week?' I would ask him, gingerly.

'Have you?' he would snap back.

I worked when I could, but I was so ill most of the time that I could barely rely on my own capacity to earn; he needed to come through for me and the baby.

'My mum says she hardly even noticed she was pregnant till she went into labour,' Dan informed me over dinner one evening. I had dragged myself off the sofa where I had been lying with a basin on the floor. I was dizzy and still nauseous, but I had been determined to make us dinner and to sit down with Dan, making some effort to act like the loving young married couple I wanted us to be.

'Is that right?' I replied, too weak to even argue or rise to the bait.

I had made us pie, potatoes and peas, and I was desperately trying to eat, knowing that I had to build my strength up or I would never get through this pregnancy.

Dan had finished his food and my plate was almost full.

'Mum says you're just lazy,' he went on.

'Does she?' I replied – I was so exhausted, but I was trying to keep the peace. She wouldn't have said I was 'lazy'; she would have said I was a 'lazy fucking slut' who didn't deserve her precious boy.

'Christ – you're full of great conversation, aren't you?' Dan noted. 'And . . . if you don't want that, I'll have it . . . you're taking forever.'

With that, he scooped my food onto his plate and laughed. I hadn't eaten all day and there was nothing else in the house, as he hadn't given me any housekeeping money that week. Dan disappeared that night and didn't come back for a few days. Without him there, I didn't have the energy to make any sort of effort.

When he did return, I still hadn't managed to keep any food down and was feeling incredibly faint. I heard the door open as he walked in. He came over to where I was curled up and looked shocked.

'You look terrible,' he said.

I muttered my thanks.

'No, really, Tracy – are you ill?'

'Just pregnant,' I reminded him.

'I don't think this is right,' Dan finally said. 'You do look really, really unwell.'

By the next day, it was obvious that I was getting worse. I struggled to the GP, who told me to go straight to the maternity hospital.

'This isn't acceptable at all,' he told me. 'You don't need to suffer – but you do need to eat; I can't even tell you're pregnant by looking at you.'

He wasn't the only one who was shocked at how frail I was. When I arrived at the hospital, the booking midwife tutted at my appearance.

'What have you done to yourself?' she said. 'We need to get you sorted, young lady.' The nurses built me up with Complan and tried to give me medication for my sickness, but I was terrified in case it harmed the baby.

'Will it be safe?' I asked, time and time again.

'You need to think of yourself,' they kept telling me. 'You'll be no use to anyone unless you start looking out for you.' But I simply couldn't risk my baby's health, so I never did take the medication and just soldiered on. I was kept in for a few days but when I went home, I found that nothing had really changed. Dan's violence continued, but I was so immature and emotionally naive that I almost accepted it. I certainly had no idea where I could go for help and support. I stayed at home a lot once I got out of hospital, reading all I could about babies from books I borrowed from the library. I painted murals on the walls, jungle scenes with parrots and monkeys. I also read as many books as possible that I thought would 'improve' me, whatever I could lay my hands on; I knew that I had to keep busy or I would start to dwell on things.

We actually moved in with Dan's dad and stepmother about halfway through the pregnancy. Cathy was such a nuisance, and lived so close to us, that I needed to get away from her, but there were also problems in the building and some subsidence which made it unsafe. Phil – Dan's dad – and his new wife had just had a baby themselves, a lovely little girl called Milly. I helped look after Milly when her mum went back to work, and I was delighted to get the chance to build up some real experience. The flat was in a pretty hideous part of town, though – it was the early 1980s and Edinburgh was well on its way to becoming the HIV and AIDS capital of Europe. There were junkies everywhere, police sirens constantly blaring, and the underground passage we used was dangerous even during the daytime. I couldn't even take Milly out for walks, so I spent my time reading more as well as learning what I could about feeds, sterilisers and bathing a newborn. We had joined a waiting list for a council house and, when I was eight months pregnant, we were given one in the Pilton area of Edinburgh. Although the new neighbourhood was still rough, it was our own space, and I was glad of that.

I went into labour while I was alone in the flat one night. Dan hadn't been home since the previous day, and for all I knew he could be lying drunk in a gutter somewhere. The pain was getting stronger and more frequent, so I called a taxi and was taken to the maternity hospital. I left a note for my husband: *I'm having the baby – please come to the hospital as soon as you can!* it said, and I prayed that he would get there quickly.

I was given a little room in the labour suite where midwives came in and out all night. I was so young and completely unprepared for any of this, despite all the books I'd read.

I felt as if I was asking the midwives the same questions over and over.

'Am I nearly there?'

'Will the baby come soon?'

And, time and time again, 'Is my husband here yet?'

I wondered whether they thought I was lying, and there was *no* husband. I was left on my own for hours at a time, with staff only popping in every now and again to measure how far I had dilated, not really giving me any information. After thirty hours of labour, there was no baby and no Dan. I couldn't believe that I was having to do this alone and the terror increased when the obstetrician informed me that it was all taking too long.

'You'll need a caesarean,' he informed me curtly, as if it had all been decided. 'We need that baby out.'

I was terrified. 'No! Please, let's just wait a bit – is there nothing else you can do?'

The thought of a major operation with no one by my side was awful, but the doctor was adamant. 'If you want this to end well, you'll do as you're told and agree to this,' he said.

The thought of a C-section on top of everything I'd been through was just too much, but what else could I do but agree? As they took me down to theatre, I couldn't stop crying and felt sure I was about to have a panic attack. At that point, just as they wheeled me in, my body was convulsed with pain.

'Something's happening!' I screamed.

One of the midwives shouted, 'It's coming now!'

Before I knew what was happening, I was in the operating theatre and bearing down. Within minutes, I had given birth there before they could begin the section. It was as if the baby had taken over and decided that things had gone on for too long.

I looked down at the crying creature who was placed in my arms immediately, and I forgot the fact that Dan had missed all of this. I forgot everything for a moment.

My baby – my little boy.

I called him Joe. He was the most perfect creature I had ever seen. His mouth was like a rosebud, his hands tiny and soft. I counted all of his toes, all of his fingers, and was amazed that I could have produced him from my broken body. I couldn't take my eyes off him, but a midwife gently uncurled my hands from his tiny body and said they had to do the usual checks that happen immediately after birth.

I lay there, euphoric that I had brought such a perfect little person into the world.

'Why don't you get some sleep?' the midwife said, 'then we'll get you back to the postnatal ward.'

'Will Joe come with me?' I asked.

'Well . . .' she replied, and her eyes flickered over to where an obstetrician was blocking my view of my little boy.

'Is he all right?' I asked, panic fluttering in my chest. Why was this taking so long? Why hadn't they given him back to me?

'Let's just get you settled,' she said, pulling a cover over me and getting ready to wheel the bed back to the ward.

'No!' I shouted. 'Give me my baby! Give me Joe!'

I saw another midwife wrap him in a blanket, tightly swaddling him up, as the obstetrician came over to me.

'Joe's not very well, Tracy,' he explained. 'He has severe pneumonia and needs to go to Special Care. In that unit, we'll keep him in an incubator and do all we can to make him better.'

I didn't even get a chance to know him before he was taken away. I wanted to hold him close, keep him near me, smell him, touch him, but it wasn't to be. It felt like his illness was my punishment. Mum had always said I was useless, and now it seemed that she was right. I wanted to breast-feed but was told the most I could do was express with a machine. It was so impersonal, so cruel, and not at all how I had imagined my first days with my baby would be.

Dan didn't show up until the next day. He breezed into the maternity ward as if it was perfectly acceptable to leave his wife and child alone for so long.

'Where is he then?' he asked.

'He?' I asked. 'You don't even *know* what I've had – you weren't here.'

'I just . . . well, my mum's always said you'd have a boy, so I thought . . . did you have a wee lassie?' he said, looking disappointed already.

'No, Dan, I had a boy,' I replied, wearily. 'You have a son – Joe.'

'Well, where is he?'

'Special Care.'

'What's that? Is there something wrong with him?'

'He has pneumonia – as you would have known if you'd been here. He's ill, Dan, he's really ill.'

I started to cry as all the emotion of what had happened just hit me. Dan got me out of bed, and we went up to the unit to see the baby. When we got there, the midwife gave us some good news.

'Joe's doing much better,' she said, 'he'll hopefully be out of here tomorrow. You'll have to stay in a bit longer so we can keep an eye on him, but it's looking much more promising.'

Dan rolled his eyes. 'Fuss over nothing,' he said. 'All that drama!'

He barely looked at Joe that day, and was obviously keen to get back to his mum and the pub so he could play the proud dad rather than actually being one and supporting us both. A few days later, once Joe was with me, but still being monitored, Cathy waltzed into the ward, stinking of booze and grinning from ear to ear. I assumed she was just happy about the baby but, as she came closer, she said, 'I've got a surprise for you!'

Standing at the ward door was my surprise.

My parents.

Cathy had been tracking them down, desperate to find out all the things I didn't want to tell her. She'd finally pieced lots of little bits together, many of them from Dan, who had thought nothing of betraying me. Cathy had found Mum and Dad back in the UK, living in Army barracks about thirty minutes away from me. They'd been there for two years – Dad had taken voluntary redundancy due to Mum's ill health – almost as long as I'd been back in Scotland. The thought that they had been so close sent a chill down my spine. They could have gone anywhere – why here? I'd been trying so hard to make a new life and they'd been there all along.

'So,' Mum said, 'you've made me a granny, have you?'

I was speechless. Joe was ill, Dan was useless, Cathy hated me, I was dealing with post-pregnancy misery, and the mother who had rejected me was standing hand in hand with my abuser as if I had made it all up. I hadn't seen her for years, I hadn't seen him for years, and now they were here. It was one of the hardest situations I had ever been in – and that was saying something.

Mum walked over to the plastic cot where Joe was sleeping.

'Looks nothing like you,' she said to me.

'I don't think he looks like Dan,' added Cathy, lips curled in distaste, never missing a chance to paint me as promiscuous.

215

'Can you leave, please?' I whispered. 'Dan – please stay, but everyone else, can you go?'

'Typical!' snorted Mum. 'Hasn't seen us for years, keeps our own grandchild from us, relies on a *stranger* to track us down, then kicks us out as soon as we get here. Fine – I don't stay where I'm not wanted, but I can assure you that I will not have you lock me out of that child's life. I'm his granny – and I intend to be in his life whether you like it or not, madam.'

With that, she flounced out, Dad at her heels, having never said a word.

'You're an ungrateful little bitch,' hissed Cathy, 'but I'm on to you – I'll work out what you're hiding. Come on,' she said, gesturing to Dan that he should follow her.

My husband shook his head at me and headed for the door.

'No!' I called. 'Please stay – it'll just be us and Joe.'

'You're kidding?' he snorted. 'You just don't see how hard Mum's trying, do you?'

I was left alone with my baby and a flood of unwelcome memories.

I got home a few days later, with Joe, but couldn't stop thinking about things, overthinking them perhaps. Mum had made it very clear that she wanted to be a granny to Joe, but the thought of her and Cathy having anything to do with my little boy was vile; I certainly couldn't even countenance Dad being left alone in the same room as him. I started to feel very down, very low, and I couldn't connect with Joe. I had thought that the only thing necessary was that I wanted my baby, I knew nothing of postnatal depression, but I would soon become an expert. In some ways, it's not a surprise that I fell victim to it. As well as the huge hormonal surge that comes post-birth, my body was reliving some terrible memories. Research now shows that pregnancy and childbirth can be enormous triggers for abuse survivors, but I didn't know this – I just thought I was a failure.

It was a nightmare. I thought I was losing my mind. I felt that I was letting Joe down but there was nothing I could do about it. It was my son who suffered the most because I distanced myself from him – I only attended to his daily needs such as washing, winding and feeding, because they were all I could bring myself to do. I felt as if I was wading through treacle. I became obsessed about the cleanliness of the house. I was constantly washing the curtains and made my hands bleed with so much cleaning. I needed that blood, I needed the pain, because it meant that I felt something. During these moments, I did think to myself, *Mum would be proud of me! Look at how clean my house is!* I thought that I was to blame for the way I was feeling, I thought it was all down to me as usual. I feel ashamed about that time of my life to this day and no amount of counselling would ever change that.

When Joe cried, I screamed terrible things to myself.

'God, I wish you weren't here!' I'd yell to the tiny baby. 'No wonder Mum didn't want me if I was anything like you!'

I would also think that maybe Dad was right and that no good would come of telling Mum what had happened. I thought that this was the punishment he had warned me about. Mum always said that I was useless and now I knew she was right. I couldn't even give birth to a healthy baby, nor could I feel natural love for him.

I wouldn't answer the door if anyone knocked. Keep yourself to yourself, I heard Dad's voice saying in my head. He seemed to be in my head a lot during those days. Was he still controlling me, I wondered? Could he manipulate me from afar? Dan was hitting me a great deal by that point, but I felt as if I was in a dull haze, not really experiencing things, just existing each day. As life with Joe went on, and he got bigger, my self-harm continued. Dan would see the house was clean, but he didn't seem to notice the price. He never mentioned the cuts on my hands and arms, the damage I was doing to myself. I was so tired all of the time. The only moments of energy would come when I cleaned frantically, but afterwards I would fall into an exhausted stupor. Dan was still as lazy as ever, drinking away money we didn't have and shy of an honest day's work.

On nights when he was out with 'friends', I would lie in bed pretending to be asleep as soon as I heard his key in the door.

'Are you awake or what?' he asked one evening.

I could smell the alcohol on his breath – from every pore of him – and continued to lie still. After he had asked me the same question a few more times, I felt him trying to turn me over.

'Tracy!' he hissed, as he flopped my body onto its back. 'Tracy!'

When I didn't answer, it infuriated him. 'Are you taking the piss?' he shouted, and he slapped me hard across the face. 'You're my fucking wife – wake up!'

My hands went up to my face to protect myself just as Dan's hands went down my body. He ripped my knickers off and I immediately knew then what his intentions were. I tried to kick him off me but he was too strong. He prised my legs apart and forced himself on me.

I had been here before. Too many times.

I couldn't believe that now, in my own home, a wife and mother, I was being raped again. Again, by a man who should have loved me, who should have wanted to protect me. Was this all I was ever destined to be?

It seemed to last forever, maybe because he was fuelled with drink, maybe because time had stopped for me as my past came back. After he was finished, I got another slap and he flung me from the bed before passing out.

Stumbling, I ran a bath, thinking back to all those other times when a man had forced me to bathe after subjecting me to appalling abuses. I lay in the boiling hot water for a while; I think I was in shock. I was certainly distraught. I had only recently admitted to Dan some of the darker details of my childhood, after he had confronted me once Joe and I came home, about by my reaction to my parents' reappearance – I hadn't told him too much, for fear of what he might think of me and what he would relay to his mother, but I had told him enough to make him understand why I never wanted to see Mum or Dad again. I had told Dan what my dad had done to me and he was now doing the same thing.

Is it going to start all over again? I asked myself.

Is he going to use that to control me?

I slept on the couch that night. In the morning, when Dan rose, he saw my cut lip and the bruising.

'My God, Tracy – I'm so sorry!' he cried, the tears springing all too easily from his eyes. 'It'll never happen again.'

'What?' I asked. 'The slap or the rape?'

He looked horrified.

'I didn't rape you!' he protested. 'I just wanted to make love – it just got out of hand because I'd had a few drinks and you were being awkward. I'd never rape you, darling, I'd never do that. What sort of man do you think I am?'

'I don't know, Dan,' I told him. 'I don't know any more.'

However, in my heart of hearts I suspected he was exactly the same type of man as my father. And I was right. Just as my father had never looked back once he broke down a barrier of violence or abuse, the same went for Dan. He continued to rape me, but the excuse changed. No longer did he say it was because he wanted to make love and things 'got out of hand'.

'You're my wife,' he'd say, 'and you'll do exactly as you're fucking told.'

When he forced himself on me sexually, it gave even more power to the flashbacks. Were they the same person? I mused. Was I married to Dad? Was he telling Dan what to do? My saviour had become my tormentor, in much the way that my father should have been my protector. I was caught in a repeat cycle of my father's abuse at the hands of my husband. There were such parallels between my past experiences, and I couldn't get over the sense that I was now trapped in a loop, dealing with the same issues.

My nightmares were worse than they had ever been. Memories and flashbacks brought Dad's hands to my mind. I could feel his touch and the smell of him would come during my dreams, but also as a flood into my thoughts throughout the day. It was as if he was standing there beside me, watching me squirm and trying to ignore the horrible feelings and visions of him. In my lucid moments, I would hold my baby and just cry for what seemed like hours, promising him he would have a better life and that nobody was going to hurt him – which was ironic, because most of the time I tried to avoid him. I felt those were my honest times though, I felt that I did truly love Joe but that I wasn't worthy of him; he'd be better off without me. I just wanted to lie down and sleep, never to wake up again. I never used the word *die*. That to me would have been so final; I said and thought 'sleep' instead. I wanted to sleep forever. I felt so tormented by my past and I could see no way forward.

I worried that if I couldn't cope, I would have to leave Dan, leave our house, and go back to my parents. This was what finally jolted me into action. I couldn't bear the thought of Joe being with them, so I finally went to the doctor. He gave me Valium, sleeping tablets and another antidepressant. I was scared to take them, scared to give up control, but even more scared to do nothing and lose Joe.

It took me eight months to recover. A long, long eight months. I know that PND is an illness, but I still feel shame and anger that I did that to my baby. No matter how hard I tried, I couldn't control my thoughts or my memories, nor could I prevent the emotional neglect I visited on my son. I know now that the re-emergence of my parents at the hospital, thanks to Cathy, was a huge trigger for me. It couldn't have come at a worse time. I had had such hopes for my life with my baby, yet it seemed to me that Joe had become ill as punishment for my past. When my tormentors walked in, it was as if all my negative thoughts were given form.

When Mum started coming round to our new house (Cathy had 'kindly' given her our address), Dan offered me no protection. She was determined to play the granny role and I was too ill to resist. I pretended to be really happy and in love, to be the proud, loving mother for two reasons – one, to show her how a mother and a wife should be and, two, to show that I wasn't stupid, I could do something for myself. When she was there, I pretended everything was perfect – I loved Joe, I was a perfect mother, Dan was a perfect husband, we had a fairy-tale life. I wanted her to think I had managed it – I had managed to make a wonderful life for myself.

I didn't mention the abuse to her again at that point, because doing so would have shattered the illusion of perfection. Abused little girls don't grow up into perfect wives and mothers, do they? Nasty little liars grow up into nasty big liars, and I feared that she wouldn't believe this happy-family charade I was trying to sell her if I raked up the past again. The irony was, of course, that I *was* lying this time. I knew she was just there for Joe, but I was desperate for her to notice that I needed her too, just as I'd always been. The only thing I said which did allude to the past was that I would never allow Joe to be left alone with Dad.

'If that's what you want,' she said icily. It was hardly the response of a woman convinced of her husband's innocence.

I rarely saw him when I visited, but when I did walk into their house I felt sick, and sweated, running hot and cold in seconds. My belly would churn and the horror of it all would come back to me. It was, of course, a completely different house, but that didn't seem to matter; it was the sense of him, the knowledge that he lived there that affected me. It was always arranged that he wouldn't be there, so that took the edge off it in some small way, but I think I always felt that Mum would renege. As time went on, the boundaries were pushed – he would be there when I turned up, but would leave straight away or go into another room. It wasn't enough – I wanted no sign, no smell, no glimpse of him. Thinking back now on how I felt then, I realise that when I did visit, there really wasn't anything lying about that reminded me of him; no books or clothes or shoes, even the ashtray had been cleaned. I'm not sure if this was a deliberate move on Mum's part to

223

'remove' him from the house when I was there; if it was, it was the only decent thing she did.

Dad was a real loner in Edinburgh. As far as I'm aware, he had no friends, living by his own mantra of keeping himself to himself. He had started a job as a security guard and I think he loved being back in uniform, it gave him an identity again. But he was behaving erratically at this time, behaviour which soon began to worsen. There was no conversation or eye contact if we ever misjudged the timings of my visits and inadvertently crossed paths. I was anxious every time I saw him; the past hadn't disappeared, it had just faded when he wasn't there. I was feeling stronger on the medication and was seeing Mum perhaps once every couple of weeks. She only paid attention to Joe, and I realised that she would never have come back into my life if he hadn't been dangled in front of her by Cathy.

Life went on. Dan was drinking so much that we were constantly short of money. He was a charming drunk in the pub, standing everyone rounds, but a dark cloud descended when he got home – and I was an easy target. His mum wasn't helping matters.

'Are you hanging around today, Little Miss Too-good-for-us?' she asked one day, when we took Joe for a visit.

I burst into tears – Dan had raped me that morning and it was all too much. I didn't expect kindness from her, but she couldn't even be civil. They both started to laugh uproariously. It reminded me of when Mum used to make fun of me with Gary – I had gone from one spoiled boy and his adoring mother to another.

Dan was rapidly losing the ability to keep his temper in check. One night, we had been to see an Elvis tribute act, a rare night out for us both. I'd felt uneasy all evening, as Cathy was looking after Joe, and I let my guard down. I would usually have been wary about disagreeing with Dan. When he said that the act had been 'crap', I had replied that I thought he was quite good before I knew what I was saying.

He grabbed me by the throat and hissed, 'If I say he's fucking crap, he's fucking crap – understand?'

I nodded as much as I could, given that he was close to strangling me, and he let me go after seeing how terrified I was. I walked on but Dan was walking more slowly, almost deliberately staying behind me. All of a sudden, a bottle flew past my head and, as I turned, he ran up to me and punched me full on the face.

'Never, NEVER, contradict me like that again, bitch,' he yelled.

He grabbed my wrist and dragged me home. When we got in, he shoved me into our bedroom, before I could even see Joe, told me to stay there, and then went to the living room where Cathy was waiting for her golden boy. I cried myself to sleep, wondering how this would ever end.

The next day, he was full of apologies, as violent men often are. It was the drink. It was my fault. I needed to watch what I said. It was only because he loved me so much that he wanted me to stay in line. We could be so happy if I would only behave.

'I can't live without you,' he wept. 'I need you so much, Tracy, and I'm terrified that I'll drive you away.'

I consoled him. I had nowhere else to go, and I always wanted to believe him when he was like that. As Mum would have said, I'd made my bed, now I needed to lie in it.

CHAPTER 12

THE FUNERAL

Dan's cronies were always hanging round the flat. They all drank and fed each other bravado as well as booze. None of them worked and it was a horrible atmosphere. When they were there, it was almost a relief to go to Mum's – despite fearing seeing Dad there, I knew that, if I had to, I could just keep walking.

Life was hard, but I had got over the postnatal depression when I found myself pregnant again. Joe had just had his first birthday when I went to the doctor, knowing in myself that I had conceived once more, although God knows what the circumstances of the conception had been. I was terrified of so many things, but I knew I could never terminate the baby so just made the best of it.

My second pregnancy was a walk in the park compared to the first. Again, Dan played very little part in it. He was there at conception, but then opted out for the next nine months. I was scared while I was pregnant and for a while after the birth because I thought I would get postnatal depression again, and I dreaded the feeling of letting this baby down the way I felt I had let Joe down. Surprisingly though, things were smooth in that department. Dan was still violent throughout the nine months, but he stopped raping me (proving that it had been a choice all along), and the birth was much easier. I had no depression this time. To some extent, I was living a separate life from my husband. He was drinking constantly and I was a full-time mother to two little boys. Joe and Ryan were the centre of my life, and I just accepted the abuse from Dan as part and parcel of what went on. That sounds so unlike the person I am now, but I was desperate to have a normal life in those days and, sadly, normality for me meant violence, abuse and emotional torture.

The fact that my parents were in my life did not mean I had forgiven or forgotten at all. Mum barely spoke to me when I went round, focusing on the boys and only ever engaging with me if she wanted to ask something about them. I still avoided Dad. In fact, I knew very little about their lives – they weren't even the ones who told me that Gary had joined the Army. I sometimes bumped into Mum's sister Fiona, who lived close to them, and I got more objective information from her. Mum never said anything of note, but Auntie Fiona believed that Dad wasn't adjusting to civvy street very well and was feeling the strain of Mum's illness, which had been flaring up once more. Although she had been diagnosed properly at last, her body was rejecting the medicine she had been given and she had been advised to have her spleen removed. When Mum was in hospital, I did visit at times, but I also got updates from Auntie Fiona who said that Dad was acting in a very odd way.

'He's driving on the wrong side of the road,' she told me. 'He's drilling dozens of holes in the wall panels of their house, filling rooms with hundreds of stolen toilet rolls, talking to himself, and claiming that he's being watched. I've no idea what's happening to him,' she told me.

I never believed anything Dad said, but I didn't see any reason Fiona would lie. On one occasion, when we were both visiting Mum, he ran into the ward where Mum was (he wasn't even meant to be there at that time) with a demonic look to him.

He was ranting, repeating over and over again the same things.

'They think they'll catch me, but I've fucked them up good and proper!' he said.

'Who? Who are you talking about, Harry?' asked Fiona.

'You know, you know who I'm talking about! I couldn't find them in the walls, but I know they're there somewhere!' He was walking around, dribbling, laughing, talking to himself, and didn't seem to recognise any of us.

Fiona tried to settle him. 'Get a doctor, Tracy,' she told me.

I had to leave and get Joe from toddler group, and Ryan was getting a bit weepy too, but I stopped a nurse on my way out and asked that someone be sent to look at Dad. That night, I went back to see Mum, as I hadn't really managed a visit that afternoon, given Dad's ranting.

'What happened when I left?' I asked her.

'Oh, he's been sectioned,' she replied, casually.

'What?' I gasped.

'They've taken him away to the Royal Ed,' she went on. The Royal Edinburgh Hospital. I couldn't believe my ears. That was the local 'loony bin'.

'He's schizophrenic, you know,' said Mum.

I shook my head.

'You must have known,' said Mum, talking to me directly now, and looking me in the eye.

'Known what?' I asked.

'About him – about him being . . .' she made a twisting gesture at the side of her head. 'Not *right*, there's something not right with your dad.'

I didn't know. I really didn't. I always assumed he had chosen to be the way he was, to do those things to me – did this mean that he had no control over what he did? Was this his 'Get Out of Jail Free' card?

After a few weeks – weeks that brought even more confusion to me – I was finally told by a doctor that Dad had been schizophrenic for some time.

'How long?' I asked.

'It's impossible to say,' replied the psychiatrist.

'How long?' I pressed. 'It's important. It's really important. How long?'

'I'd be guessing . . .'

The Funeral

'Then guess – but make it as accurate as you can,' I begged.

'A number of years,' he answered.

'What's the number?' I pushed.

The doctor sighed before replying, 'Ten to fifteen.'

Not long enough, I thought.

When I went back to Mum she asked if they knew what had 'caused' it.

'Maybe it's his badness coming out,' I said, wearily.

As usual, she questioned nothing.

'We all have badness in us,' she said, calmly.

I didn't. Not when I was five and he was raping me.

The following weeks brought flashbacks and night terrors for me. I was looking after two little children, pretty much on my own, and dealing with all of this; something had to give. When Mum said one day that she thought Dad was 'stressed', I curtly informed her that stress didn't 'give' you paranoid schizophrenia. She argued with me and, when she said that her illness hadn't been easy for him, I snapped and said that her illness had a lot to answer for.

'I can't help it, it wasn't my fault,' she said.

'You could have helped some things, Mum, you know that.'

'Let's not go there,' she snapped, trying to end the conversation on her terms.

'Let's,' I said, staring her down. I told her that she had never listened, that Dad had used her illness to control me, that he had raped me for years.

'Not this again!' she shouted. 'I won't hear it! I won't hear another word!'

I left. There was no point in staying, she would never listen and I'd never get the apology I wanted. I was starting to wonder whether it mattered anyway.

Although Dad did get released, he was never well again. Mum, on the other hand, went from strength to strength. By the summer of 1985, he was taken back into psychiatric care and my life was falling apart. I knew that I had to challenge him; I knew time was running out.

I left the kids with a friend and took a bus to the Royal Edinburgh hospital. Dad was looking old and weary – although he was barely fifty. There was no easy way to start this.

'Do you remember everything?' I began.

He waffled about being in hospital before I brought him back to my question.

'Dad – I mean what you did to me when I was little.'

He avoided my gaze, and I repeated what I wanted to know, but he squirmed as if he was a toddler getting told off for being naughty.

'Sorry,' he said, grudgingly.

Was that it?

He said it again when I asked if he remembered.

'Sorry.'

Then he made an excuse about being ill, saying it was his head, saying that he was unwell. He was causing a scene, and a nurse came over to take him to his room, looking at me accusingly when she said he was upset.

I was never left on my own with him again at the Royal Ed. His 'sorry' was empty and meaningless and I have no idea whether he even knew who I was. I wanted to challenge the man who had abused me, but this *creature* was just a shell, an irrelevant shell.

Two weeks later – two weeks of hell as I tried to come to terms with the fact that I might never get closure, he was taken to a medical hospital. Ironically, Dad was complaining of feeling that something was in his throat, that he wanted to gag all the time. *I know how that feels*, I thought.

The doctors discovered that he had a tumour, but when they opened him up to operate they found he was riddled with cancer. There was nothing to do. We were told he was close to death. Two days before he died, I told him that I needed him to admit it all to Mum. I still hoped that I could be reconciled with the woman who had never loved me and I foolishly believed all that stopped us from having a healthy relationship was this one thing.

'Why did you do it?' I said to him over and over again, feeling as if I had regressed, feeling like a child. Mum came in, demanding to know what was going on, and I truly thought he would give me what I needed. He looked me in the eye and said only one word.

'Tracy.'

That was it.

No apology, no explanation.

I was in bits. I couldn't sleep, couldn't eat. I was barely a mother to the boys and I just knew I had to do something.

I'd tried everything else, I told myself – there was only one thing left.

I went to the hospital and saw, not my dad, but a tiny, shrivelled-up old man, half-dead already. I looked at him and knew that my hatred would consume me if I gave it that power. I needed to give myself a chance. This wasn't about Dad – or Mum – any more; this was about me.

'Dad?' I whispered. 'It's over, isn't it? It's all over.'

There was no reaction.

I took his hand.

'Dad – it's OK, it's done. I'll be fine,' I told him.

There was no reaction but I hope he heard me. I said goodbye and left. He died a few hours later and with him went my chance of ever receiving a real apology.

I went home and held my babies, sobbing into them as they remained oblivious. For the next couple of days, I was on autopilot and then, one afternoon, the phone rang.

'The funeral's organised – there's nothing for you to do,' Mum said.

'Are you sure?' I asked, wanting, as always, to be of some use to her, to do something she would appreciate. I wasn't grieving for my dad – how could I? – but I did still harbour a small hope that Mum would reach out to me and that we could be together at this time. Now that he was gone, perhaps she would feel free to be a real mum to me without the cloud of him and his attitude towards me hanging over us both.

'What could you do?' she snapped, making it very clear that things would go on as usual. 'I've got Gary – it's all done.'

The Funeral

As always. She had Gary so there was no need for me.

'I could phone people, arrange things, get you whatever you need?' I offered.

'You've been told,' she snapped. 'There's nothing you need to involve yourself with.'

He was still my dad though and, even though I had often wished him dead, I had thought there would be something I could do at this time – something *normal.* I wasn't trying to *involve* myself in something which had no link to me, in something I had no business with, I was simply offering to help my mother bury my father.

'How are you getting there? How are you getting to the crematorium?' I asked.

'How do you think?' she replied. 'The family car's coming at ten.'

I waited to hear what would be expected of me – would I be asked to be at Mum's house early, would that offer an opportunity for us to move towards each other in some way? Would she sit between her two children on the way there? As these thoughts went through my mind, her words filtered through.

'Do you hear me? Do you hear me, Tracy? We'll meet you there.'

'What?' I asked. 'Where?'

'Oh, for God's sake, pay attention! We'll meet you there. At the crematorium. We'll get there in the family car, you make your own way.'

It was official – I wasn't to be in the family car; she didn't even consider me real 'family', it was just her and

Gary, and whoever she chose from her brothers and sisters to take precedence over her other child. After the conversation with Mum, I kept changing my mind about whether I even wanted to go to the funeral. He was nothing to me, not in any real sense, not in the sense a loving father would be, but I tried to convince myself that I would get some pleasure from seeing him go into the fire. So I decided that I definitely would go, and there was still that little, persistent (stupid) voice in my head saying, *maybe Mum will need me tomorrow; maybe it was the grief talking and she'll reach out to me. I can't miss that chance. I can't.*

The next day was beautiful, sunny and dry without a cloud in the sky. As I dressed, my thoughts started jumping about again. I was glad that Dad had finally gone, I couldn't deny that, and I was relieved that he couldn't hurt me again. Even if the damage he had inflicted would last a lifetime, there would be nothing new, no more. Perhaps even, without him there – a malevolent presence in all of our lives even if there was very little contact – Gary would tell Mum the truth and then, with the words being spoken by her own golden child, she would finally believe everything I had told her. We could all move towards making some sort of fractured – but better – relationship and perhaps I could finally heal.

I left my two boys with a friend and took a bus to the crematorium. It wasn't too far and it gave me a chance to try and pull my thoughts together. I was completely alone. I hadn't seen Dan for days – he was probably at his mother's house and he had made no attempt to comfort me or even offer to attend the funeral.

The crematorium wasn't busy the day they burned him. I knew that being cremated wasn't what Dad had wanted at all, and I took some pleasure from that. In fact, I had often heard him say, quite explicitly, that his worst nightmare was to be burned. He had wanted to be buried and it had preyed on his mind. He hadn't said that dying was the worst thing he could think of, just the method of getting rid of him after it had happened. As I walked towards the crematorium, I wondered why this had been important to him. Had he thought there would be weeping hordes at his graveside for years to come? Did he expect me to lay flowers there on anniversaries? What, Dad, *what* did you think those anniversaries would have been? Would I bring roses for the first time you called me a whore? Would there be a big bunch of chrysanthemums for the day you raped me, or the tenth time, or the last time? What type of flowers say *I hate what you did to me*?

There were very few people there: his mum, his brother and sister-in-law, his sister and brother-in-law, and one friend. I wasn't surprised – who would mourn that bastard? None of his workmates turned up, nor did anyone from his Army days. Mum was there with some of her siblings – but, actually, Gary wasn't there. He had decided that 'business' elsewhere was more important. I knew this would hurt Mum, but I also knew that I would go to her in an instant if she needed me, despite it hurting even more that there had been no place for me in the family car, even when Gary wasn't around.

I don't know what I wanted to see in the faces of the other mourners (it didn't really look as if anyone was 'mourning' but I guess that's what the official name would be for all of us), but there was nothing anyway. Everyone just had nondescript looks on their faces. There was no weeping, no wailing, no emotion really. A man was dead – a man who very few of them knew the true side of – but they all looked as if they were waiting for a bus. They were all in black suits, raincoats, Sunday best; many of them probably had special funeral-wear that they were taking out of the wardrobes much more frequently as they all aged, but there was nothing other than the sea of black to indicate that a funeral was about to take place.

I stood apart from them all, waiting for the sign – which often seems invisible – that would indicate we all needed to go inside. No one seemed to be looking for me; they all kept their heads down, smoking and saying very little. As my eyes scanned the waiting few, I noticed two women together. They were from our time in Germany – and one of them was Agnes, and I recognised the other woman beside her as Diane, the lady who had comforted me when Mum had made me do the splits.

Both women in front of the main door looked just the same as they had when I had seen them last, so many years ago, although Agnes looked about ten years older than she actually was, I think due to the clothes she was wearing. They were dowdy and old-ladyish, not reflecting the strong, confident woman I'd known in my youth, and I wondered if something had happened to change her. Diane looked no different – she was a completely different shape and size to Agnes, and they looked quite odd together. I'd had no idea that Mum was still in touch with either of them, and I really hoped that I'd get a chance to talk to Agnes at some point.

Watching them, and the other mourners, I felt completely and utterly alone until I realised someone was standing beside me, tapping my arm gently.

'Tracy! Tracy!' the woman hissed, trying to bring my attention back to the moment. It was my Auntie Marge, one of Mum's sisters, who I hadn't seen for years. I was relieved that someone had made a move towards me, and smiled at her warmly.

'Oh, Tracy, I'm so worried about Valerie,' she began hurriedly, in a low voice. 'Her health's still bad, you know. She's a fragile woman, a very fragile woman, and the worry . . . the worry's doing me no good at all.'

'I'm sure she'll cope,' I said. 'She hasn't been in hospital for ages, and she seems to be fine.'

'No – no, she isn't fine at all,' Marge went on. 'She's been acting . . . strange. Very strange, Tracy.'

'What has she been doing?' I asked.

'Well, yesterday, I went round to see her, to see if she needed anything, and she was sitting in the living room, surrounded by all these photographs of her and your dad.'

'That doesn't seem odd,' I pointed out. 'She was probably just thinking about old memories.' Old memories, I wanted to say, that would be very different from those in my mind.

239

'No – it wasn't *right*,' Marge confided. 'She had ripped them all up.' My auntie reached into her black handbag and brought one of these photographs out. 'I took this from the pile when she went to make a cup of tea.'

It was a photograph of Marge, her husband and Dad taken when they had visited us in Germany in 1973. Mum had ripped off the part that Dad was in so that my auntie was left with a picture that showed only her and her husband. Marge went on to tell me that there were dozens like this, all with Dad removed.

'Did you ask her why she was doing this?' I queried.

'I did, I did indeed,' she nodded. 'She said that she didn't want any memories of him. I told her that she had ruined some lovely photos and your mother just replied that she didn't care. Her exact words were, *They couldn't be good if that bastard was in them.* I asked her where the ripped parts were, the parts with Harry in them, and she said that she'd burned them all.'

'Has she done anything else, Marge?' I wondered out loud.

'His car; Harry's car,' she answered.

Dad had loved his car. It was a garish green Nissan with stripes in a different shade of green. It was obvious and tacky, but he had adored it.

'She told Gary to get rid of it – scrap it. She didn't want it sold, she didn't want any "dirty" money from it, she said. She never wanted to risk seeing it again, she just wanted it gone, scrapped. So, he did – Gary took it to the scrap yard and it's been wrecked. She's burning him, Tracy – even when Gary pointed out to her that Harry would never have wanted that, she said it was her choice, and she was happy with it. There's to be nothing, Tracy – she's not putting his name in the Book of Remembrance or getting a rose shrub in his name. It's not right, Tracy, it's not right at all.'

Shaking her head, Marge walked back to the main group but I couldn't help thinking that it *was* right, in fact, it was the only 'right' thing I could think of my mum doing for years. The fact that she had wanted to erase him from photographs, that she had burned the pictures of him, that she never wanted to see his car again, have no memory of him anywhere, gave me hope. Maybe she would come round – maybe she was already on her way to facing up to the truth.

As I walked closer to the door, everyone started to file in to the hall. Finally, Mum made eye contact with me. She shot me a glare as she held on to her brother's arm, going up to Agnes and Diane and whispering something to them. When I got into the hall, behind everyone else, I guessed what she must have said. I wasn't welcome beside her and she had made sure that the two women from those long-gone days were filling up the remaining seats in the 'family' pew.

I sat directly behind Mum but she didn't acknowledge me. At one point, Agnes started to stand up, but Mum pushed her down into her seat again, making it quite clear that she had no wish for me to be by her side. As I waited for the service to begin, I looked at all of those family members from both sides, including my own mother, and wondered what they were thinking about the man in the coffin in front of them. Was Mum finally facing up to the truth? Was she having a silent conversation in her head with the man she knew had abused her child?

I felt disconnected from it all.

In fact, I was glad. I wanted to stand as far away from the man who had been my tormentor as I possibly could. The second row wasn't far enough back for me. No, it wasn't my distance from 'him' that was upsetting, it was the fact that, yet again, Mum had managed to make this all about how deep she could dig the knife in. Even at a funeral, she could still make me feel as if I wasn't fit for her to wipe her shoes on. I had, naively, thought that at this moment in her life she might have needed me – and like the fool I was, I would still have gone to her with open arms if she had shown any affection; but just like other times in my life, she pushed me away.

The only hymn I can remember is 'Abide with Me' – there was no reading, there was nothing memorable at all. The minister doing the cremation said that Dad was ex-Army and had served his country well, that he was hard-working and a proud man. I was never mentioned. It was as if he didn't even have a daughter. It was all over quickly and I rushed outside, where it was still warm and sunny. As I lit up a cigarette, Agnes gave me a hug, which took me unawares.

'I'm so glad that you're married and doing well, Tracy,' she told me; I could only assume she had got this information from Mum, who must have packaged it up in a manner acceptable to her, preferring just to accept the version I was presenting her with than to dig any deeper. 'I've often thought of you over the years . . .' her voice trailed off at that point, and she squeezed my hand. I didn't tell her the truth about my life; I'd always liked Agnes and could see no point in dragging up the past with her. She, after all, had tried.

'I'm sorry that you couldn't sit with your mum,' she said, awkwardly.

'It's fine, really,' I lied.

'Valerie needs her friends at a time like this,' Agnes went on, as I nodded in vague agreement. 'You know what it's like.'

'It doesn't matter,' I assured her. 'Some things never change.'

'Well, your life has, Tracy, and that's good, it's really good.'

That was the last time I ever spoke to Agnes. Even at the funeral meal, Mum made sure that she distanced me from everyone, surrounding herself with a wall of friends and siblings, making sure that everyone knew I was an outsider. The meal was at a local miners' welfare club.

The miners' club was a large place with a big dance hall, complete with a wooden dance floor, and deep carpeting around the outside where the table and chairs were. It could hold over a hundred people, which only highlighted the small size of the funeral party, and had a bar, a disco ball hanging above the dance floor, and spotlights above the seated area. There was a boardroom and a large lounge with circular tables. The carpet was dark red with small yellow circles on it, with a gluey smell which reminded me of new paper money. The walls were covered in flock wall-paper, burgundy and cream. The tables had white table-cloths and were set out with knives, forks and spoons, and cups and saucers. A buffet was waiting, which consisted of sandwiches and sausage rolls.

I found this choice of venue strange too, as Dad had always hated the place; it was as if Mum was doing all she could to rub his nose in the fact that she was in charge now. I've often thought that, if we had been close, maybe we would have bonded over those decisions, gaining strength from the realisation that he could no longer lay down the law. The club was a place Mum went to when she wanted to play bingo locally. Also, her brother was a member, so I'm sure she would have got it on the cheap.

At the meal, I sat between two of my uncles, my mother's brothers; both of them had come back from abroad for the funeral and knew nothing of what Dad had really been like. They tried to keep everything 'normal', starting up those strange conversations which people have after someone has died, in which every word means very little, and clichés abound.

Uncle Chris began by saying, 'Such a shame for Harry – barely fifty and gone, just like that. It's just as well we don't know what's ahead of us.'

I could relate to that comment.

'Aye, he certainly got a dull one, the poor bugger,' rejoined Uncle Rab.

'Nice bloke, though,' Chris went on. 'I always liked him when he was courting Val. At least he got his twenty-two years in.'

This was in reference to Dad's full Army service – the twenty-two-year period would have assured him a good pension.

'I don't think he quite got to that,' said Rab. 'He'd put in for voluntary redundancy – he was six or seven months shy of it, I think.' He was right; Dad hadn't quite made it and no one was sure why he hadn't lasted that extra bit of time.

'Really?' asked Chris. 'How strange – you'd have thought he would have held out. Ah well, Valerie seems to have had a happy enough life, she'll get through it.'

'He'll be missed. Good bloke.'

'Aye, that's for sure – good man. Time to raise a glass, I think.'

I became infuriated. These people really didn't know him, they didn't know what he had done, that he had stolen my childhood, ripped a family apart – to them, he was a good guy and they felt totally justified in singing his praises. I couldn't handle it. I looked around at all these people, who thought they knew him. I looked at my mother, surrounded by friends and family, while I sat on the edge, alone and rejected. The years of frustration and pain bubbled up inside me and I couldn't contain my feelings any more.

'Drink to him?' I spluttered. 'That's a first – no one ever sat with him or went out for a drink with him! A good bloke? Going to be missed? You lot don't know the half of it. The man, if you can call him that, was an utter bastard and nobody knows it better than me and my mother!'

Looking around, I realised I had attracted the attention of the others, even Mum, but that didn't deter me. My dad's family looked horrified.

I stood up.

'Go on, the lot of you. Raise your glasses to someone you never saw and certainly didn't know. You'd have spat on him if you'd known what he was really like.'

'Tracy, shut up and sit down,' hissed Uncle Chris. 'You're upsetting yourself and your mum!'

'Upsetting Mum? That's a laugh,' I continued, feeling the heat of my argument through my whole body. 'She spent all day yesterday cutting up every photo that the bastard was in! Cremated him when he wanted to be buried, has the meal here when he hated the place . . . upset her? Don't make me laugh. Upsetting myself? Never – not now he's gone. May he rot in hell. Here's a toast to the Devil – because he's got his work cut out with good old Harry.'

With that, I walked out. I could hear Uncle Rab say, 'Don't mind her, she's just upset; she'll be OK.' Other people were muttering and whispering behind their hands. I didn't hear what was being said, but could sense the low murmur, which I knew was about my outburst. I had a quick glance back at Mum. She was just staring blankly into space. She didn't look upset or alarmed at my outburst.

I went to the bus stop and headed home.

The Funeral

I hadn't cried during the service and I didn't feel like crying now. When the hymn was being sung, all I could think was *the bastard's got away with it* and I still felt that way. I know that we're told never to speak ill of the dead, and I know that many people can forgive, but it had all just burst out of me. I was angry that I would never get justice and that he had died thinking he had got off scot-free. I kept my emotions bottled up all the way home, knowing that if I started crying now, I might never stop.

When I did unlock my front door, it all poured out of me. My body was heaving, I couldn't stop shaking – but I knew I wasn't crying for him, not for my father. I wasn't even crying for myself, not the Tracy who had just buried her Dad. I was sobbing for that little girl who would never get justice. I was glad he was dead, but I wished he had died years ago, before he'd had a chance to hurt me, or at any point when he was in his prime, rather than as this pathetic, broken old man. I wanted justice, I wanted some sort of revenge, but I knew I would never get it in that form. The tears finally stopped, as did the shaking, and all I was left with was the revelation that no one would ever save me, and no one could ever change the past. All I could do was try so hard to move towards a time in my life when I could think of my parents and what they had done to me without bitterness, without it hurting me even more. I knew I was a long way from that, but I needed to hold onto the hope that, one day – not today – it would happen.

CHAPTER 13

ONLY A DAUGHTER

Things were going from bad to worse with Dan, and our entire relationship was falling apart at the seams. He hadn't been paying the rent, so we were evicted the week after Dad died. Dan did a runner at that point and I came back one day from a trip to the park to find everything in the front garden – the cot, all our clothes, every single possession. There was nowhere for me to go. I'd had no contact with Mum since Dad died, and I would have felt odd staying with her anyway even if she'd allowed it, so my only option was to go to a women's refuge. It was safe and it was a roof over our heads, but it was soul-destroying too. Living there with two little children so soon after Dad's death made me feel like a complete failure.

Dan reappeared shortly after, completely unrepentant about what he'd done to us. Somehow we were lucky enough to be given another house (I think because the boys were so young), and the whole cycle began again. He was hitting me and raping me regularly – but now he was also taunting me with the details of my abuse. During the rapes, he would repeat back the things I had told him, my trust repaid by hearing those horrible words over and over again which Dad had used on me. The horror was compounded by the knowledge that Dan was getting sexual gratification from all this, and actually seemed to like to hear what I had been through. It was at this point that I also discovered he had given me a sexually transmitted disease. Until that point, I really hadn't believed he'd been cheating on me on top of everything else, but there was no denying it when the test results came back after I had been to the doctor complaining of feeling very ill. My darling husband had given me gonorrhoea.

About a month after the funeral, I plucked up the courage to visit Mum. I hoped that maybe she had now come to terms with the reality of me and Dad, now that he was dead and she had been given some time away to think about it all. After his death, I truly thought she would be more supportive. I had hoped she would have called me by then, but there had been no contact, not even when I knew she was back from her holiday. I took the boys with me, and knocked on the door. There had been so much going on in my life since I'd last seen her and now, more than ever, I just wanted her to listen and support me. No matter what, no matter how little love or support I had ever received from her, there was still this small hope inside me, still this automatic impulse to turn to my mother.

'Oh, it's you,' she said, with her usual disappointed expression. She turned her back and walked into the house.

I followed her to the kitchen where she was already laying out biscuits and drinks for her grandsons. She spoke to them, but ignored me.

The boys started playing with a few toys she kept there for them and I tried to make conversation. I was getting little more than a grunt here and there, so thought I'd just ask the question which had been bothering me since I'd spoken with Auntie Marge.

'Mum,' I began, 'why did you rip up all the photographs which had Dad in them?'

She narrowed her eyes, finally looking at me.

'He was a bastard and I don't want anything of his left in this house.'

It was the answer I wanted.

'You accept it then, Mum?' I said. 'You've finally got it, haven't you? You've finally believed me!'

She flew off the chair, knocking it to the ground.

'I don't want to discuss this! I've told you before, Tracy – I DO NOT want to talk about this,' she shrieked.

'But, Mum—' I stuttered.

'NO! This is MY house, MY rules – you can get out now if you're not going to respect my wishes. I want no reminder of him but I DO NOT want to discuss it. The photos are gone, the car is gone – everything. Let that be an end to it.'

I'd had that response from her in the past but had hoped there would be a breakthrough this time. It's only now that I realise *I* was a reminder to her of what a bastard her husband had been, I was a constant thorn in her side because of that. What he had done to me pushed us further apart rather than bringing us together, but I didn't see it then, I didn't have the distance.

I took the boys and left. As I walked home, tears in my eyes as I pushed the baby and Joe trotted at my side, I thought I must be imagining things. I was so upset that I couldn't quite work out whether I was actually seeing Dad's distinctive green Nissan being driven up the long road I was walking, about two miles from Mum's house. There were no two cars like that though – I couldn't be mistaken.

Gary hadn't got rid of it. He had lied to Mum (and everyone else), not taken it to the scrap yard, presumably sold it and kept the money for himself. I don't know what happened to that car in the long term, or whether Mum ever found out, but I know that, even if she did, she would have forgiven him in a heartbeat.

About five months after Dad died, I finally found the courage to split with Dan. I was feeling better physically in that the medicine for the STD had helped, but, even better, he had kept away from me sexually when he knew I had it. He told me I was disgusting, even though it was his fault and I had never been with anyone else. The time away from the constant sexual attacks meant that my head was clearer. One day, while he was out drinking, having not been back for three nights, I put all of his things into black bin-bags and threw them out into the street. I called the council and they changed the locks for me, then I barricaded myself in, waiting for him to come back and kick off.

I hid behind the door with the boys, singing to them as I tried to distract them from their dad outside. He was screaming obscenities, and also shouting that he would never let me go.

'I know you, Tracy!' he yelled. 'You need me – you need a man to be there, you know what you are and I know that you will never be strong enough to walk away!'

He was wrong. After a few hours of his verbal abuse, he tired, being more drawn to the pub than his family. When he left, he said that he would be back later to 'burn me out' of the house. I believed him. I didn't even think that our children meant that much to him; he only thought about winning the argument, as he saw it. I wasn't going to be caught by him, so I packed all I could and went to a home-less shelter on the opposite side of the city. They were kind to me, but resources were limited; like the women's refuge, it was a desperately sad place, but, again, it was all I could get so I was grateful.

When we had been there a couple of days, I went to see Mum.

'I've got something I need to talk to you about,' I began.

'You've split up with whatsisname,' she said. 'I know, he was here. Anyway, listen – I've got something to tell you too.'

This was unusual. She rarely told me anything and, even allowing for her lack of interest in my life, I was still will-ing to take anything I could, so I looked keen at whatever she was about to say.

'Remember I went on holiday?' she asked. I nodded. Of course I did, it was so soon after the funeral that I wouldn't forget. 'Well,' she went on, grinning, 'guess what?' I opened my eyes wide and tried to look intrigued. 'I met someone! I met a man!' she squealed like a teenager. Was this really my mother, I wondered? She couldn't wait to tell me all about him.

She couldn't have said anything that would have surprised me more. My mum with another man, months after Dad had died? Surely it was a joke?

'Oooh, we clicked straight away, you know,' she said, ignoring my look of surprise. 'He's from here, he's local, and I've been seeing him every day since I got back. He's called Brendan and I think I might be in love!'

Brendan was twenty years older than her, divorced with three grown-up children and a lot of grandkids. He was short and retired, handsome and 'distinguished-looking', apparently. It wasn't all rosy. She told me that Auntie Fiona said he was a gold-digger who hung around holiday camps looking for widows, which sounded about right to me, but Mum was having none of it. She had never spoken to me like this before. It was as if she was seeing me as a real person, someone to confide in, and I did like it, even if I had reservations about Brendan.

Within weeks, they had moved in together and Mum was giddy every time I saw her. I should have seen what was coming next, but I was naive as usual, so when she announced, less than eight months after Dad had died, that they were going to get married, I was shocked. I still hadn't met Brendan – Mum always found excuses when I suggested it – and I was concerned at how fast things were moving, and told her so.

'I should have known,' she moaned. 'I should have known that you would never want me to be happy. Always a daddy's girl, weren't you? Always his little angel.'

What could I say to that? His angel? She knew what she was doing, I'm sure of it.

'Well, let me tell you this – no one, *no one* will stop me! Brendan loves me and I love him. He's a good man and I deserve a little bit of happiness in my life. Now piss off,' she shouted. 'I don't want you here if you can't be happy for me. I don't want to look at you, take those brats and piss off!'

She couldn't be reasoned with. I took the boys and left.

Although I was now living in a new flat, Dan had managed to track me down. One night when the boys were in bed, he caught me unawares. He had been there a few times before and spent all of the 'visits' screaming up at my window, shouting obscenities and making a nuisance of himself. The new neighbours hated me and I couldn't blame them. I had brought noise and disruption to their quiet street, and every time I spoke to someone, it didn't matter how polite or friendly I was, I could just tell that they associated me with the disturbances caused by Dan.

That night, I heard all the buzzers in the stairwell go off and when my own one was finally pressed, I heard a muffled voice, which I didn't recognise, saying that he had forgotten his key and could I let him in? I was busy with housework and did so without my usual carefulness. Within seconds, Dan had kicked down the flimsy door to my flat and was coming at me, hatred on his face and murder on his mind.

'I'm going to fucking kill you, you fucking bitch!' he roared. 'You'll fucking pay for this – you'll pay for ignoring me, locking me out, taking my kids!'

With that, he got me by the throat and started squeezing. I could hardly breathe and all I could think of was my boys, what Joe and Ryan would do without me if I let Dan win. My hand scrabbled around behind my back and I felt a knife on the washboard. I grasped it and held it up in front of Dan.

'I'll use it! I will!' I wept. 'If you don't leave, I'll use it.'

He let me go, backed away and stood at the opposite wall from me.

'You wouldn't fucking dare,' he laughed. 'If you'd have been able to stab anyone, you'd have stabbed your fucking dad – or maybe you just enjoyed all of that a bit too much?'

I didn't really think about my response – I just threw the knife. It missed him by a mile and lodged in the wall. Dan took it out and, screaming, ran at me. He grabbed my hand, laid it flat on the kitchen worktop and skewered it with the knife. The pain shot through me and I started to panic. The blood seemed to be everywhere and he was laughing like a maniac.

'Call an ambulance! Please get me an ambulance!' I begged, but Dan just started laughing again. 'Stay here with the boys then!' I shouted, rushing out into the street. I thought that one of the neighbours must have called for help when the fight began, as I saw an ambulance coming up the street. I ran into the middle of the road to stop it and the vehicle screeched to a halt.

'Help me! Please help me!' I shouted. They took one look at the state of me, one look at where I lived, and drove away. I went back to the flat – Dan had run off by now – still dripping blood even though I was holding my hand in a tea towel, and dialled 999. When I was put through, I gave my name and address. As I waited, I heard someone say to the operator, 'That bloody family! Always one drama or another – put the phone down, leave them to it.'

They did. They hung up. No one would help; Dan and his family had such a reputation that I couldn't even get the emergency services to help. I actually complained about what happened and there was an enquiry. Years later, the report found in my favour and I was given compensation but, that night, I needed help and it was nowhere to be found.

The boys were crying alone in their beds. I slept with them that night, holding them tight, even when I thought I was going to faint from the pain in my hand. I got stitched up at the walk-in clinic the next morning, but the damage had been done. Some tendons had been sliced through, the delay had made it all worse, and I would have countless operations over the years in an attempt to rebuild my hand. I didn't prosecute; I just wanted Dan to disappear. Thankfully, he did for a while – perhaps he too was scared by the intensity of the violence and by what could have happened, but he also found me again some time later after I'd moved again. In fact, I'm pretty sure that Mum told him where I was, as very few people knew and that's just the sort of twisted thing she would do.

'I only want access to the kids,' he told me when I opened my door to find him standing there one night. 'You could just let me in now.'

'Let you in! I've been running away from you – I don't want you anywhere near my children.'

'They're my children too – and they deserve a father.'

'They deserve a better father than you,' I shot back.

'I'll get a lawyer – I'll get them off you, Tracy.'

He stood there arguing for what seemed like hours. I knew the boys were asleep but I was terrified that they would appear behind me. Eventually, I gave in. I was scared in case he meant it – what judge would let them stay with me? I was useless, a horrible person.

'To begin with, you can have them on Saturdays,' I said. 'I'll meet you in town at the bus stop and I'll pick them up there again. You can have them from twelve till six.'

After a month, Dan started coming to meet the boys at the bottom of our close. I was just out of hospital after having had further surgery on my hand. He came three times, and on every occasion, Joe would be sitting at the window waiting for his dad, all excited and happy. Then, on the fourth weekend, Dan never showed – or the next week, or the next. He had found a new girlfriend and wasn't interested in the boys any more. He had only asked to see them when he had nothing better to do. I stopped all of the visits then. Joe still remembers sitting at the window watching and waiting. He doesn't speak to his dad now and I think that hurt will always remain with him.

I never missed Dan once he left my life for good; he had beaten and raped me, he attacked me with a knife, he had given me a sexually transmitted disease, he had nearly broken my son's heart. I tried to convince myself that I loved him in the beginning when I saw him as a kind of protector, but he turned out to be a long way from that.

After a while, there was no money to feed us. I couldn't do anything really, given my injury and we had nothing coming in. I decided to swallow my pride and ask Mum for help. I hadn't seen her since I had expressed concerns about Brendan, but one night, with all our bellies growling from lack of food, I took the boys and walked to her house.

Brendan was just leaving as I got there.

'Hello!' he said, in a warm and friendly manner. 'I was wondering when I was going to meet you – good timing, but I'd best be leaving, really. You'll know why!' He winked and stood aside to let me in.

'Oh, for Christ's sake – what do you want?' asked Mum. 'Turning up just to spoil things; typical of her.'

'That's a bit harsh, Val,' said Brendan.

'No, it bloody well isn't! You don't know her, Brendan – if it isn't one thing, it's another. Now, what is it you want? I'm trying to get ready for my hen night.'

'Hen night!' I exclaimed. 'I didn't know. I had been hoping that you'd be able to lend me some money for groceries. Things are a bit tricky just now. I've never asked you for anything before, Mum, but I really need your help.'

'It's my hen night!'

'I know – you said,' I told her. 'Look, forget it, but, this wedding – well, it's a bit soon, isn't it?'

It's bugger all to do with you, that's what it is. Me and Brendan are happy and well suited.'

'As suited as you were with the last one?' I asked. With that I stormed out.

I was back staying in a refuge by this point, so scared was I that Dan might change his mind and come back to the flat for the boys. About an hour after I got there, there was a knock at the door. I peeked through the spy hole and saw Brendan.

'Here you go,' he said, thrusting a bag of shopping into my hands. 'I got your mum to get you these but . . . erm . . . she wants the money back some time.'

He seemed embarrassed, but nothing about Mum surprised me any more. He asked if I was all right.

'Is your nose a wee bit out of joint because Val's remarrying?' he wondered.

I laughed and said that wasn't it at all. She could do what she liked as far as I was concerned.

'Are you able to come to the wedding then?' he enquired. 'That would be nice.'

'Brendan, I didn't even know when the wedding was until tonight. I certainly never got an invitation,' I told him. He looked confused, but wished me well as he left.

I heard nothing from Mum, but when I was given my new council flat, it turned out to be only two minutes away from where the newlyweds lived. Brendan actually came round and asked if he could help with any painting and decorating, moving furniture or generally helping out. I asked him if Mum knew he was doing this, and wasn't shocked when he said he thought it best to keep it quiet. He was just passing and popped in to see if he could lend a hand. I said I had plenty of people to help (I actually didn't have a soul), but as he left, he said it would be nice if I could pop in to see them sometime with the kids.

After I had been there a week, I did go round and Brendan was there. Mum said, 'This is your new papa,' to the boys, and I stopped her, saying that they'd be calling him Brendan.

Mum glowered at me and Brendan noticed the look. 'Don't worry, Tracy,' he said, 'I'm not trying to fit into your dad's shoes; Brendan's just fine.'

I liked this man. 'Don't you worry,' I told him. 'Nobody would want to fit into his shoes, I can assure you.'

'That's enough!' squeaked Mum. 'Don't speak ill of the dead!' I only stayed long enough to have a cuppa. I just nodded and smiled at the right times and was so glad to leave.

I went up again the following week. This time, Brendan spoke more than before. He was telling me how great Mum was with his kids and that they had taken a shine to her, especially his daughter and her three children. He mentioned that they had all been out for a meal and was sorry that I couldn't make it and that maybe next time I would go too. I was very confused and Mum was looking away from us. I told him that I hadn't been asked.

'Val – I thought you said that Tracy didn't feel up to going?' he asked.

'No, you must've picked me up wrong. I saw she wasn't looking well and I assumed she didn't want to come along,' lied my mother.

'Well, I must be going deaf in my old age!' chortled Brendan. 'Not to worry, Tracy, next time; it's going to be great for the two families to meet!'

As time went on, it became clear that Brendan was a very nice man but that Mum was lying to him about our relationship. One day, she said something about not keeping secrets and I couldn't keep quiet any longer.

'Well, that's a change!' I said to her. 'You're good at keeping secrets, aren't you, Mum? If there aren't any these days, why not tell Brendan what really went on in our family? Go on!'

'Don't be so bloody stupid! Stop trying to cause trouble!' she replied.

'What's going on? What do you mean, Tracy?' asked Brendan.

I took a deep breath and it all came tumbling out. 'I was sexually abused by my father for years. I told Mum and she ignored me, said I was a liar, and did nothing. Nothing! Then when I did speak out I was sent to boarding school, someone else had to save me.'

'She's lying! That didn't happen at all!' shouted Mum.

'Val, you told me Tracy went to that school because she

needed to be challenged educationally! You said that you and your husband scrimped and saved for years.'

'Her? Her – clever? That's a joke – what challenges would she need?' snorted Mum.

'Mum – how many times and how many excuses are you going to hide behind? Brendan, it's the truth, even my brother knows the truth!'

'None of it is true, Brendan. She just loves making me unhappy, it's just her way of getting me back,' said Mum.

'Getting you back for what?' asked Brendan.

'Leave it, Brendan. I don't want this mentioned again and, as for you, Tracy, I don't want to see you again. Ever.' With that, she turned and stormed away.

'My God, I'm so sorry, Tracy,' said Brendan. 'I'll talk to your mum.'

I didn't see Mum again for two years – and at about the same time, I started drinking. At first I thought I was glad she was out of my life, I could move on without having to make her face up to the fact of what Dad had done to me. I didn't miss her during those two years, and couldn't even have cared less when she walked past me in the street one day, dramatically turning her head the other way. I found it easier to hate her and blame her as one of the people who had ruined my life. Her absence was felt, but only because I wanted to scream and shout at her, make her see what my dad had made me become. I hated her for not believing me and for turning her back on me. When I started drinking, I was blaming everyone but myself.

*   *   *

Life went on, but it was all a struggle. I was coping with pain and still going into hospital regularly for surgery on my hand. My tendon needed to be replaced and the doctors were attempting to slacken the scar tissue that hurt constantly. I needed to go into hospital to have my fingers straightened for three to four days at a time. Money was still short, I was earning but it wasn't a lot. The kids were getting older and more demanding in the way that kids are when they realise there are designer clothes in the shops and all their mates have these things; only brands will do.

When the kids were a little older, I got a job as a book-keeper in an office. They were at school by this time, but I still needed someone to help out so that I could work, and an acquaintance at the office suggested her nephew Ewan.

I invited Ewan over for a cup of tea to introduce him to the kids, and they seemed to like him, so the arrangement was made that he would become my babysitter. He would collect the boys from school and give them their dinner. It was hard for me to trust him, but, to be honest, it was hard for me to trust anyone. However, another problem was beginning to take root in my life that would have skewed my judgement anyway. I don't really know why or how my dependency on drink started, but it did. In the past, when I was young, I had gone out and had a drink with Dan, but I only associated it with being social back then. When I started to work, I also became better at making friends. They all went out at weekends to the local miners' club and I tagged along. I was feeling alone, desperately alone, and that my life wasn't going anywhere – these drinking nights out at the weekend made me feel a little better. It wasn't the company I was in, it was the alcohol. I was able to go home and flake out, with no sleeplessness, and no dreams or nightmares when I did sleep.

After a couple of weeks I started to go out on the Sunday night as well as Saturday – with friends and to the same place. Prior to this I'd had Sunday to get over my hangover. Ewan would come over and feed the kids, but I soon began to find myself suffering on the Monday morning, feeling fuzzy-headed and sickly. My work never suffered, I was just slower at it.

Some time later still, on a Monday, I bought a bottle of cider from the off-licence in my street on the way home, and downed it once the kids went to bed. When I woke up the next day, I felt fine – and from then on, cider was the poison for me. It soon became a pattern and I was drinking every night of the week. It wasn't long before I needed more and more drink, because I was getting used to it; I needed more to be able to sleep at night.

At weekends, I would let the kids go out to play. They would return home hungry and I would prepare them some lunch, while Ewan would make a meal for them before the weekend babysitter came and we all went out, as he was part of that group at weekends too. Ewan and I became very friendly, but he would go straight home after our nights out as I didn't want him to stop over; there was no physical relationship with him but I did wonder if that would change. At the time, however, I was grateful for any kind of support and comfort, and in the light of my previous experiences of sex, I was not particularly looking for a sexual relationship; I was also just too caught up in my drinking.

Prior to the start of my alcohol abuse I would take the boys out to the shops and then spend some time with them in the park. On some weekends we would go to a funfair near our house. I would allow them to bring their friends home to play in the flat and the garden. That was all changing now and, when I drank, Ewan had to act as a mother more than a babysitter. Before my drinking began, I would come home and get their dinner, make sure they did their homework and sit and watch a bit of telly with them, then they would have their baths and go to bed with a kiss from Mum. That had all stopped. I started to drink during my lunch hour, and now, by the time I got home at night, Ewan had the boys ready for bed. I rarely interacted with them, too busy wallowing in my own misery.

I was alone within myself. I thought I was completely unlovable and I really didn't know which way was up. The pattern of thoughts my mind followed during my drunken nights was usually the same: I would try to mask my addiction from myself, delude myself by making myself promises that my life was going to change – I would get a better job, send my kids to a private school, make sure they didn't want for anything, show my mum how great a mum I was – then sit and wish Mum dead. Around and around I would go. I was hurt, I was angry. I preferred to live life drunk as it numbed the pain from the memories. I hadn't really faced up to my past, I hadn't discussed it with anyone who had been able to help me, and I know now that I was being self-ish. It served my purpose to forget, to have a comatose sleep where I didn't dream. I was like Jekyll and Hyde – nice and quiet in sobriety but terrible in drink, where I hated the world and everyone in it.

I thought I was immune to everyone actually seeing what I was, but there were signs that people did know. My boss once said, while I was stinking of drink, 'Get this sorted or you're out.' I had made quite a few mistakes with the payrolls I dealt with, but I'm sure he was telling me to get *myself* sorted rather than to correct my errors in the accounts.

'You're drinking far too much, Tracy,' Ewan would tentatively suggest. 'The kids are beginning to notice.'

'Rubbish!' I snapped. 'I only have a few once in a while.'

'Really?' he replied. 'Then why did Joe just say to me that he wanted you to help him with his homework but you couldn't as you hadn't had your cider yet?'

That cut me deeply but I just responded by being a bitch to Ewan. I think I was trying to make people hate me – maybe I wasn't comfortable with a happy life. I didn't think I deserved it and I was always thinking it wouldn't last anyway.

During those six years when I drank, I hardly gave Dad a thought. Somehow I put it to the back of my mind, or so I believed. I still had some nightmares that reminded me of him but they were less than in the earlier years. When I was drunk I pretended to myself that I was happy, but I couldn't keep that pretense up sober. In reality, the more I drank the more depressed and unhappy I became, and then I would be angry at this in my sober time. It wasn't long before I became a very angry young woman constantly, one who hated the world and everything in it, yet I continued to drink.

My kids began to run wild, skipping school and getting into fights. I wasn't oblivious to this but I deliberately ignored it and let Ewan handle it all. We were living together by this stage but it was a strange relationship. We didn't have sex, and there was nothing physical about how we were with each other. I didn't mind in some ways, as I liked Ewan and liked how he was with the boys, but I still dreamed of that fairy-tale ending.

Ewan was quite happy with this setup too, and he was a lovely man, so when he proposed to me, I decided to accept. The wedding took place on a glorious summer's day. It was very different from the experience I'd had with Dan, as Ewan had money – and taste. He organised a full white wedding with a Rolls-Royce and vintage Jaguar to take us to the church. My sons were pageboys dressed in beautiful kilts; they were really excited to be getting a new 'dad' and they adored Ewan. At the ages of nine and twelve years old, they were in awe of everything – the cars, the church, the food at the reception. I was dressed in a long gown with a full train and veil; I felt so special. It was as if all my dreams from childhood had come true – a white wedding to a shining knight who had saved me from myself. I got lost in the day as I was the centre of attention, the blushing bride with six flower girls and my boys beside me.

Ewan was from a big family, and they were all friendly, so I was able to have the day I had always dreamed of.

'You look amazing,' he told me as I stood beside him at the altar, and I believed him. It was all perfect – or almost. I had called Mum to ask if she would come but she had refused, saying, 'You need to apologise to me for a hell of a lot before I'll even consider that.'

I couldn't do that – I couldn't apologise to her when she was the one in the wrong, and had been for years. Someone said that they saw her at the back of the church but that she had left before the end of the service.

There were about forty people at the wedding, but hundreds at the reception. We had a 1970s themed party and I was really happy for the first time in a long while. Ewan's mum and all of his sisters were there – all eight of them! I didn't have many family members there, just a couple of aunties and uncles, but they did comment – as did others – about how 'sad' it was that Mum hadn't made it. A few people did ask if she was ill again, and those who didn't know her were soon given her medical history. I didn't mind that – I'd rather they thought she was poorly than she had chosen not to attend. She had let me down yet again, which was pretty much what I expected from her.

As the reception went on, it was time for me and Ewan to slip away, to spend our first night as a married couple in a local hotel. I had been doing some work for the hotel's owner and the stay was a gift to us. We weren't planning on a honeymoon as such, but this would be time away from the boys. We were both pretty drunk and when we got into the room, Ewan threw himself down on the bed, laughing.

'I can't see much happening tonight, can you?' he joked.

It didn't bother me, and as I looked into the mini-bar, I could hear him snoring.

There was no sex on our wedding night and, to be honest, I can't say that I was in love with him either. But I did like Ewan an awful lot. I believed that I could trust him, both in relation to me and to the kids. He was gentle and kind, really the only man I had ever felt safe with. I thought it was because he loved me as a man should love a woman, but I think now that I was only ever a good friend to him. I don't blame him – it was my fault, my stupidity for thinking it was more. We staggered on for a year – no sex, but a lot of kindness and a fondness for each other that meant a great deal to me – but my world came tumbling down and I ended up back in a women's refuge after Joe caught Ewan with another man in 1995. At the age of thirty-three, I was about to go through my second divorce. I gave up my work at that point to be there for the kids, which was ironic because by this time the boys were actually able to get their own meals and do their own things. All it meant was that I had more opportunities to drink as much as I could lay my hands on.

After we had moved to a new flat and away from Ewan, the door rang one day and a neighbour told me that Ryan had stood on a bottle and cut his foot badly in the garden. I was drunk as a skunk and told the bloke that it would be fine, then closed the door and went back to my bottles. I conked out due to the drink, until the doorbell rang again some time later. The man had taken Ryan to the doctor's, where the nurse had stitched his foot. I was confused, as I couldn't even remember the guy coming to the door in the first place. I felt so ashamed, and so embarrassed for my son and myself. It helped give me the kick up the backside that I needed. The realisation came that I was turning into my mother, ignoring my children and blind to their needs. That evening, I didn't have a drink for the first time in years and I vowed not to drink again – of course, I did drink again, I didn't stop altogether, but I managed to get my drinking down to a bottle here and a bottle there, usually at the weekend, rather than every night. I was hell bent on making it up to my kids; even today when I think about this time I am utterly ashamed of myself.

It was a month or so later that I saw the advert in the window of an old fire station about an adult learning project and from that point, I swapped drink for education – I was just as obsessed, just as addicted. From the moment I saw the notice for a group called '2nd Chance to Learn', I felt as if there was an opportunity for me. The poster said that I would gain confidence and self-esteem, two things I lacked entirely. I made an appointment to see the organisers and was given a meeting with a lecturer, who also taught at Edinburgh University.

'Why do you want to come back into education, Tracy?' she asked.

All I could say was that my education had been cut short and that I had no qualifications to speak of. She was really supportive and, before I knew where I was, I had joined seven other people on the course. It was a good little group, all of us were single parents looking for some sort of interaction, I think, whether it was educational or social – we all needed support in one way or another.

After a couple of weeks, I was so engrossed in my new studies and the homework I had to do, that I never even contemplated a drink. It was as quick as that. I felt healthier, more alert and active. I learned that I could drink socially and didn't have to rely on it.

My course focused on history and sociology. We had group discussions about case studies, we talked, we discussed, and we achieved a resolution to any problems that were flagged up in the studies. This, I think, helped me to sit back and dissect problems, and to look at where to put the emphasis in an argument. It made me think about my own life objectively too – I started to try and see myself as a case study.

Although I was a little shy, I soon made good friends, friends I still have today. Lasting friendships were formed, based on trust, not only with the other students, but with the tutors too. I was happier and was beginning to feel as if I was walking taller. There was an actual physical change in me: no longer was I stooped with my eyes averted from others. I was turning into a different person. The kids loved the fact that I was back at 'school' and they even tried to help when I had homework.

'This is what you were meant to do, Tracy,' one of my tutors said to me one day.

I laughed and tried to brush it off.

'Don't pretend – you love learning, you know you do. Embrace it, use it to be the person you want to be.'

She was right, I did need to accept that I was good at it. My past was still there and still coming back at me, usually in my nightmares or if I reflected on anything to do with family. I studied psychology and sociology when I moved on to the next stage at college and often studied families. Education stimulated me, helped me mix with people, gave me motivation and handed me my self-respect back, but when I read some books I realised just what type of family I had grown up in – totally dysfunctional.

Since those dark years, when I had found alcohol but not yet education, I still have a drink but I control it; *it* doesn't control me. I drink in a social environment and never since then have I had a drink in the house. I think the reason I don't drink in the house now is because I know how easy drink can take hold of you and your life, and I don't want to lose the things I have found – self-respect, education, happiness and love.

I have spoken to my sons about my lost years and asked them how they felt about it. They both thought that I was hurting inside due to what their dad had done and the miserable life I'd had with him. They (at the time) thought the drink made me happy and they wanted me to be happy. They also knew that when I was drunk they could do what they wanted and go where they wanted – they knew this and admit that they exploited it, but I should never have put them in that position. Joe took it the hardest, I think. I was called into school once about his behaviour, as he had started bullying other children. Because of my emotional neglect and lack of discipline, he had started to hang about with a group of kids that ran riot throughout the neighbourhood, and he skipped a lot of school. He assures me today that it was only through peer pressure he did this, but maybe he's just being kind to his mum.

I feel sorry for my sons more than anything, particularly in relation to my mother. She deprived them of a grandmother's love just as she deprived me of everything when I was a child. Although she seemed in the beginning to want so much to be a grandmother, she never kissed or cuddled them, never fussed over them. In fact, I could never work out why she wanted to see them at all. She was a lousy mother and an equally lousy grandmother, devoid of love for any child but Gary. She disappeared from their lives and reappeared again at different points in their lives, depending on what arguments she and I had had or how busy she was with her new husband, but I finally decided to cut her out of their lives following one occasion, when Joe had been over to see Mum for a weekend visit. I would let her take them sometimes, putting themon the bus at my side of town, with strict instructions that they were to sit next to the driver – who they knew and who would pass them to Brendan at the other side of town where he lived with my mother.

One day, Joe came back in tears.

'Don't send me there again, Mum!' he wept, running into my arms and burying his face into me.

'Why? What's wrong?' I asked, the panic rising in me. As I asked him the question, I pushed him back from me – and could see immediately what was wrong. His hair had been cut so short, he was practically bald.

'Look at my hair, Mum – look at what she's done!' he cried.

I was furious but I didn't want to let him see. 'It's only a haircut, it'll grow back.'

'No, no, I hate her!' Joe went on. 'She makes us get into the bath as soon as we go into the house and we have to change into new clothes. I'm not going back!'

A bath? A bath every time? I felt a chill go over me.

'Does she do anything else?' I asked.

'No – but that's enough!' he replied. 'She does it every week – she makes us go in the back door, not the front one, and takes all our clothes off, then we have to get a bath. She puts our clothes in a bag and gets special 'Granny' clothes for us to wear when we're there, then she changes us back again when it's time to go. I don't like it, Mum.'

Neither did I.

'It's your choice,' I told him. 'If you don't want to go back, you don't have to.'

He shook his head. 'I don't want to.'

Later that night, I dialled her number and put Joe on the phone. He told her he didn't want to come back. I knew she must have asked him 'why?' as I heard him repeat every-thing he had told me.

I took the receiver, and all I heard was, 'That's because of that little bitch.' She was talking to Brendan as she was putting the phone down. My son has never forgotten that incident and, to this day, calls her 'the Ice Queen'.

Once, when Joe was twelve, he found out through an aunt that my dad had started Post Office accounts for the boys before he died. Joe made contact with Mum and went to ask for the account books from her but there was very little in them.

'That all comes from me anyway,' said Mum. 'Your granddad left you nothing, nothing, but I've always put in two pounds when it's your birthday and your mother keeps me away. I bet she thought it was a lot more – typical of her, always wanting something!'

I was only ever her daughter. And that, that was worthless.

CHAPTER 14

NEVER-ENDING STORY

Since I wrote my first book, many people have asked me: did it help? I can honestly say, yes, it did – but not as much as this one. This book is really me, it's the warts and all, it's the hard truth, the version that I suppose I was unsure of showing people. I know in these pages I'll come across as weak to some, as vengeful to others, as insecure and unconfident all too often. It's hard to admit to all of that, but it's cathartic too.

I don't want to present a fake picture. I can't say that it's all worked out perfectly, that there have been no bumps along the way, or that I've always known I would be fine. None of that is true, and I don't think any other survivor reading this would believe me for a minute. I know that not all readers will have been through abuse themselves, but I want those people to know that you don't get fixed overnight. In fact, I'm not sure you ever get 'fixed' at all. However, the things that I thought would have broken me have made me stronger. I don't take anyone at face value. I never assume that confidence or perfection are real. I always wonder what lies beneath the surface, what the real story is, with everyone I meet.

That's why this book has meant so much. *Never a Hero to Me* was, in many ways, the framework of my story, whereas here I've been given a rare opportunity to revisit and reconsider so many of the things that made me who I am today. I think that other survivors will recognise a lot of the things that come up in these pages, not just how abusers work, but how the mind of the abused survivor functions. I hope so – I hope none of us are alone.

When I was a child, I was always so confused. Nothing seemed to make sense, and the more I tried to think about it all, the more blurred it all became. Why did Dad make me wear lipstick for him, but then tell me it was only for 'bad girls', and that, if I wore it, I would encourage boys? Why did he make me lie on a certain side of the bed and act like my mummy when I was there? If I was his good girl, how could I also be a dirty little whore? When I grew up and left home, there was still confusion, although largely in relation to the behaviour of other adults. Why had no one picked up that something was wrong? Why did I not make them see? What was there about me that was so invisible? When I allowed myself to become a victim of abuse again (and I did think I had allowed it, and I did think I was a victim, despite what the politically correct terms now are), I was disgusted with my own failings; again, the confusion arose. Why, when I had been through so much, did I let it happen again? Why was I so weak? The answer stems in part from the fact that Dad kept me so isolated and separate from everyone else that I spent much of my childhood watching other children, watching the world, through our window. This loneliness, this isolation, made me so desperate for love that, as an adult, I ignored all the alarm bells that rang in both my marriages, all the signs that things were wrong.

Feelings of isolation and loneliness ran through my adult life – they still do to some extent, even though I've found a man I love and who respects me. In my first marriage, my only friends were the people I knew through Dan. He didn't like me meeting up with workmates and tried to control me as Dad had done. My isolation from the world continued, and increased, during that dark time when my love for drink was stronger than anything else.

I feel as if I've been absent for so much of my own life. I was never really in family photographs. I can only remember one of me with Mum, and then another when I was four years old and holding that birthday cake in Singapore. I look so miserable in both of them, and I wish I could reach out and rescue the younger me – I wish I was strong enough to do that.

I am now with a man who is supportive, kind, giving and loving. We have been together for fifteen years – we have a few arguments about silly things, but we laugh at them; we laugh a lot. He knows about my life and never pressures me into discussing anything about it. If I do want to talk, he will listen, then hug me. I don't live in fear of being beaten or raped or hurt in any way. He accepts me for me, and he loves me. After what I have been through, it's a blessing that I am able to be loved at all, and that I can return that love.

I was often so angry as a child. Angry at Dad's treatment of me, not because of the sexual abuse (I was too young to really understand that), but because of the physical abuse. I was punched, slapped and kicked as if it was perfectly natural, whereas Gary escaped it all. As a teenager, I was angry at Mum for not being there, especially when I told her what Dad had been doing for years. As an adult, the real anger I felt was towards myself, especially after I had broken away from Dan. I was angry because I felt that I should not have let those things happen to me as a child and as an adult. At this time, I blamed myself for everything. I kept asking myself, why did I let this happen? Why had I let it continue? Was I truly bad? Why didn't I shout and scream louder? Did I like all of this? Was there something wrong with me? I was angry that I had never had a childhood; I realised that I had lost so much. Obviously, my virginity was something which was taken brutally and disgustingly, but I also never experienced the joy of sitting around discussing things in a group with other girls, of chatting innocently about boys while pretending we knew so much, of wondering about sex and getting it all wrong. I knew it all. I knew it all too soon.

I never had a boyfriend as a young teenager and it made me feel like an outcast. I missed out on the art of making friendships and this is so vital for any child growing up.

Some say that friendships should come naturally, but I believe that children should learn this art from their parents and peers. Dad kept me away from everyone and Mum never seemed to value her friendships, she just moved from one friend to another, looking for bingo mates.

I missed out on the rules of parenting, too. As a child I never knew that my family was dysfunctional until it was too late – I thought all parents treated their children the same as mine did. I didn't learn about parental responsibility or about normal boundaries; while my mother was absent both physically and emotionally, my father crossed so many unnatural lines.

My self-respect as a child and an adult was destroyed. I gradually gained some towards the end of my time at boarding school but, after my first marriage, I lost it all again. I had no confidence as a child or through two marriages and my alcoholism. I gained everything from education, but it terrifies me that I came so close to missing out – what path would I have taken then?

Of course, I definitely missed out on a mother's love, as a child and as an adult. When my first child was born, no words could express the depth of love I felt for him. Had my mother also felt this love when I was born? I guess I will never know. It seems to me that maternal instinct comes from within, yet she was devoid of this – why? What happened to her, and why did I pay?

I feel sorry for Mum really. I realise now that she spent all her time with her head in the sand, and lived her life without ever really being loved or giving love. Brendan loved her, yes, but I don't think he knew the real Valerie, only what she presented to him. She loved Gary, it's true, but I feel that a lot of the affection she displayed towards him was shown in order to hurt me rather than because she truly adored him. For that, I pity her. At times, I look back on my life and try to rationalise her way of thinking at the time when all the bad stuff was happening. I know she was having an awful time with her own illness, but, for the life of me, I can't see why she still couldn't be my mum. A mother nurtures, loves and protects her young, and these feelings should come naturally – but, for her, they simply didn't. She had them for her son but never for her daughter. I don't think of Valerie as 'my mum' most of the time; she is just a woman who was there and didn't help me when she could have. I have given up trying to understand why she did nothing. I have let go of the anger I felt in the past now, because that anger just kept fuelling the fire within, it made me want to hate her and Dad and it began to eat me up and make me miserable, sad and alone. If I was to make anything of myself I had to leave my past behind me and she was part of it, so she had to be taken out of my mind, before she did any more damage.

The boys have no contact with Mum. Ryan hasn't spoken with her since he was eleven. He didn't like her or her new husband so he kept away. Joe remained in contact with her while he went through a troubled period in his life and she played the dutiful granny for a little while, but the novelty wore off and she actually told him that she wouldn't be in his life as long as I was there; he'd have to choose. What kind of a woman asks her grandson to choose between his grandmother and his own mum?

My relationship with my kids has been great. I have been there for them, cried for and with them, we have laughed together and kept a strong bond throughout. I worry at times that maybe they have missed out on some things in life because I was too busy moving from one place to another, to get away from men who were no good for me, but they have assured me that at no time did they ever feel neglected or unloved. I am so proud of my children. Joe is married to a lovely girl, and I speak to him twice a week. Ryan is father to three kids who he loves dearly. I think, considering all that has happened, we are close and supportive.

Mum is still alive and married. Brendan is terminally ill with cancer so she will be alone again soon. For a woman who was at death's door for years, she is outliving everyone. I have no contact with Gary and neither do my sons. I don't even acknowledge to people that I have a brother; the only time he has been in my mind has been while I write these books. I feel nothing for him as a brother or a person.

There are still so many questions, so many things hanging over me from my childhood – and the sad thing is, there will be millions like me. As I wrote this book, I was faced with headlines and stories everywhere about another case of historical abuse. Hundreds of people were coming forward to claim that the broadcaster Jimmy Savile had abused them over the years. As calls for enquiries grew louder, there were the usual questions:

Why didn't they say anything at the time?

Why didn't they go to the police?

Why did they wait until he was dead?

Why did they only say something when he couldn't defend himself?

Why would someone in his position need to do those things?

He was a good man, he raised a lot for charity, there's no 'evidence', they're all in it for the money, because he's dead and they can claim whatever they like now.

Why didn't they say anything, why didn't they say anything, why didn't they say anything?

I've heard it all before. The truth of the matter is that no one wants to believe child abuse exists – and, believe me, even those of us who have survived it feel the same way. Why would anyone want to believe any of this? It's easier to just pretend that millions of children lie – that, somehow, babies and toddlers receive sexual abuse injuries in some other way, that children too young for school have STIs for a different reason, that little ones at nursery are acting out sexualised behaviour because of something else – because the truth is so horrific. So the culture of silencing children, and adults, continues. We are told, from the start, to shut up, keep quiet, tell no one. We are told that no one will believe us if we do tell, that we are dirty, that we are bad, that we are disgusting, that our loved ones will get ill or die or be put in danger if we talk, that we will be taken away, that everyone will hate us, that we will ruin everything. And the abuser is right far too many times.

I was so angry when my dad died, and I was so angry when I read about the Savile cover-up, for the same reason: *they both died thinking they had got away with it.* When Savile died, he was hailed as a national treasure, as someone who had raised millions for charity, and whose 'odd ways' were something to be brushed under the carpet. After all, what were the rumours and half-stories compared to the works of a philanthropist? So, he was given a flash funeral, a gaudy headstone was erected declaring what a wonderful man he was, tributes were aired – and all the time, the survivors must have thought they had stumbled into a topsy-turvy world where abusers are deified, and the victims are silenced forever. Savile died thinking he had won, thinking that his reputation was intact and that everyone believed the facade was the reality. So did my dad, and that cuts me to the core.

He *never* paid for what he did to me. I know that there will be some people who have beliefs different to my own, who will say that he did pay in his own way and that he would be made to atone for his sins. I'm afraid I don't believe that, and it would offer me no comfort even if it were true. I wanted him to atone *here*, in this life, and I wanted it to be done in a way that helped me. Is that selfish? Probably – definitely. But, after years of abuse, I don't know how else to process what happened. It was wrong – and yet I'm the one who has paid the price. I'd be willing to bet all I own that there are many people reading this book who feel the same way. As survivors of the ultimate betrayal, we're often told how strong we are – but there's no one there when we feel a million miles from strong. We're told that we're survivors (and we are) – but we'd do anything to have never had to survive this in the first place.

We're not superhuman. We've been hurt and damaged, and we just want the world to believe us and recognise that sometimes, sometimes it all comes back. We're mothers and fathers, daughters and sons, some of us have a lot, some of us have nothing, some of us are successful in the eyes of the outside world, some of us are struggling, but we're all carrying this inside and we're all asking the same thing, I think:

Why did someone feel they had the right to do that to me?

It breaks my heart to think of the thousands and thousands of people who have had to face up to what was done to them as a result of the Savile revelations. Each day, newspapers, television and websites had his face as headline news, but, worse than that, even worse than the stories of what had been done, were those who were saying that it was all made up. Those who claimed that it was a storm in a teacup, or that things were 'different' back then, seemed to be able to ignore just how much of an effect any major sex-abuse story has on survivors. The triggers are different for everyone, but equally there are words and phrases and memories that will be terrifying for so many. As those words and phrases and memories became commonplace in the autumn of 2012, I shuddered to think of the impact they would have on so many people. Those who had been directly affected by those specific crimes were incredibly brave to finally step forward, but the impact would have been wider, hitting survivors who remembered that time in their lives, or small things such as the fashions or the music, the television programmes or the trends. The very fact that Savile himself was part of the popular culture of the 1970s, that he was a figurehead, would throw many survivors back to the worst time of their lives. Many of them would be dealing with invisible abuse, abuse they had never mentioned to a living soul, but which was being played out on newspaper stands and their television screens for months on end.

I was angered by much of what came out once the Savile case started to hit the headlines because it brought it all home to me once more. We don't listen to children. We ignore their abuse when it's happening, and we generally ignore it when it comes to light. We are deterred from coming forward with our stories for fear of being sued for slander, libel, and defamation of character. We are told not to speak ill of the dead. But what of the living? What of the victim turned survivor?

So many people got in touch with me after my first book to ask for more of the story, but also to ask how I had moved past all that had been done to me. The truth is, I'm not sure it ever goes away. It hasn't for me. The memories are still there, and I still hurt when those memories break through. However, I do feel that if I had given up, if I had never broken the hold which drink had on me, or found the courage to speak out, my father would have won. He took so much from me – my childhood, my trust, my innocence – and it was vital to me that I stopped him from taking any more.

But it wasn't just Dad who did all of those things to me. Mum did too. She was capable of love, but she never loved me. She colluded with my abuser by hiding from the truth. Whenever I addressed the issue with her in later life, she made it very clear to me that it was all in the past, that she would hear nothing against her husband, even though she was happy to bad-mouth him to everyone else. Criticism of him was only allowed on her terms. If my story had been heard at that time, it would have reflected on her, and she couldn't have that. She needed to be seen as poor, martyred Valerie who had put up with so much. If it had been known that, actually, she emotionally abused her own child, and allowed that same child to be sexually abused for years, the sympathy she craved would have disappeared in a flash. It was much easier and more convenient to paint me in a bad light, portray me as a problem child, and to maintain the dysfunctional relationship between us that had always been at the heart of everything.

I wonder how many other survivors have suffered the same double heartbreak? How many of them have had a mother who compounds the sexual abuse with emotional neglect and coldness? Too many, I fear. Sexual abuse of children doesn't happen in a vacuum. The abuser grooms carefully, whether within or outside the family, always seeing something in the child that can be exploited, built upon, encouraged. A cold, distant mother is a perfect starting point – as is a mother desperate for love herself, or a mother damaged in her own childhood, or a mother so selfish that she cares for nothing but her own needs. The abuser is careful to note all of this – even when the mother in question is his own wife, the child to be groomed his own daughter.

I feel so sad for the little girl I was, for she is lost forever. I still want to save her. Parts of this book, and the previous one, could only be written because I was able to distance myself from that child; if I allowed myself to think about her from my position now, that of a mother myself, I'm not sure I would have been able to write a single word.

Do I have anything I want to say now, any advice I want to give? I'm tempted to say 'no' because I'm no expert, but you've come this far that I feel I must say something. No matter how bad your life is, there is always a way forward, always a way out. Your life is in your own hands as an adult, it doesn't belong to your abusers any more. There were dark times when I got my thoughts all muddled up. I sometimes felt that I couldn't fight any more, because if I ended up all right, that might mean that what they had done to me didn't matter. I almost felt that I needed to stay damaged to prove that damage had been done. I know now that's wrong – we need to fight and we'll probably be fighting until the end of our days, but that's what makes us survivors.

The scars are still there, the wounds will never really close – but if we take ownership of them, if we know what makes us who we are, that's the best revenge of all. That way we win.

ACKNOWLEDGEMENTS

There are so many people to thank, so please forgive me if these acknowledgements are slightly longer than usual – the main reason is that I have 'met' so many lovely readers since *Never a Hero to Me* was published. Every message I received was supportive, and the response meant a great deal to me; I finally felt that I had been believed *and* that I had been right to speak out. I want to thank all of those people first because they made the decision to write a sequel slightly easier; I could only delve deeper into my past knowing that there were so many invisible people out there holding my hand.

Here is a selection of the messages I received.

I would like to say a few things, having read Tracy's book please, if I may.

It has helped me because I grew up in the same kind of situation as Tracy. I had a physically and sexually abusive father then managed, with my increasing maturity, to cause a fuss and refuse situations. This resulted in me being put in care.

Throughout this time, my mother was unavailable, unresponsive and cold and also, similarly, out of the house or away most of the time – her own choice. She was not by any means a good mother, having her own 'problems' which meant she always put herself first, so I can identify with what's mentioned, as in total selfishness. They were two people who, in my view, should never have had a child.

However, what is really, really hard is that I was also raped as a grown woman by someone in the Forces. I find it so hard because, like you say, they are at the moment considered by society and the local towns and media as our 'heroes'. This man would walk around and gloat at what he had done to me. The police did nothing.

No one really understands the impact abuse and rape has and it doesn't matter for how long it lasts or goes on for, there are so many myths about. If it isn't ignored, it's treated like a joke.

I am glad to have read your book because it gives everyone the other side of the story. Too often, rape is blamed somehow on the victim, but how can it be? I am glad you have found peace in your life; no little girl deserves abuse. It wasn't until I saw my son at a young age, that it hit me how tiny these little people are and also how completely innocent. I don't think abused people ever see themselves as the same as anyone else, they can't live care free because of it. I hope you are happy and I hope you will feel strong enough one day to let people know what happened next. Do you still talk to your mum, for instance?

All the very best, L.

I am so gobsmacked, as I've only just finished your book, and as you left this email address I just felt the need to contact you. I've never done that before. At the same time as you were going through those dreadful things, so was I, although I was lucky I was never raped by my father.

For as long as I can remember, I was in fear of my father. I have memories of being two or three and being beaten up, thrown from wall to wall for the slightest things. As I got older the punishment got bigger and when I reached the age of ten, that's when the sexual abuse started. How I survived was my love for dance and music.

I used to sleep with the Bible under my pillow thinking God would protect me. I would pray that if I had been a good girl he would not come into my room, but years of praying to God and being good never helped.

At sixteen I went to the police, who said it would be my word against his, heck he was an ambulance man so who was going to believe me?

If you met me you would never think my first nineteen years on this earth were like living in hell. There were so many things that you touched on, from the perfume and aftershave to the cigarettes. I'm rambling now, sorry! I am a survivor and I am me. I try to be thankful that he at least gave me life. I have three lovely children and I have a good life. I wish I'd had the strength to confront him. I try so hard not to think about him but, as you know, from time to time it creeps up on you. The nightmares which make it feel as if it were only yesterday.

To think that child abuse is still happening every second around the world to many beautiful innocent children just breaks my heart. My letter could be from somewhere anywhere, from anyone, it's happening so much. I know if I read this back I will never send it, but I just feel I need to for the first time ever open my heart to someone who does not even know me.

Thank you for this and thank you for writing your book and, hopefully, for the next one, which will show how you got through it all and became the amazing woman you seem to be; for now I know I was never going through this alone, that at the same time another little girl was going through the same.

I wish you a lifetime of happiness, P.

Hello there.

I don't want to contact Tracy but I have just read her book, *Never a Hero to Me*, and it has left me wanting to ask so many questions.

Acknowledgements

As a father of two girls and a boy, and also a grand-father to five grandsons and two granddaughters, I found the book horrifying as to how a father can do that to his daughter.

I was wondering if there will be some kind of follow-up in the form of a second book as, like I said, I have many questions in my head I would like answered. Like what is Tracy's relationship with her mother now, if her mother is still alive, did she ever see her brother again, did other family members find out about the abuse?

I would really like to hear how Tracy got on after the death of her father and how she moved on to university.

Could you kindly let me know if a follow-up would be a possibility, or if it is in the process at the moment?

Thank you, G.

This was such a heartfelt, touching story; through my own experiences as a young girl I suffered abuse. Tracy's story opened up my own emotions, which I kept away because of the shame. I told my mother about what my stepdad did when I had my daughter, she didn't believe me, neither did the rest of my family. My mother is dead now, so is he. I felt no justice. I got nothing, no sorry from them both. I have my own family now, but in a twisted turn of life, my own father tried to have sex with my daughter, who was eleven at the time. I am trying to make sense of it like Tracy. Reading her story has made me realise they choose to do these horrid things. It hurts, but the pain is unreal. I would like to thank Tracy for her story, which has touched my heart, and hope she has a contented happy life.

Love H.

I have just finished reading *Never a Hero to Me*. I'm not usually the sort of person to respond to an author (I bet they all say that!), but Tracy's story mirrored so many aspects of my own that I have found myself doing so nevertheless. I would like to pass on my heartfelt praise for the book to both you and her. Having read squillions of these, I have found it to be one of the most moving and honest-feeling accounts that I have come across. It is maybe the way it is written; we appear to have a similar way of thinking, and that has made me relate to it so deeply. While our stories are different, our feelings about the events in our lives are very alike and I thought they were expressed so eloquently. I now at least don't feel quite so juvenile in wanting another childhood that would make me feel the same rosy glow that so many others seem to have! So for that at least I thank her, and would also like to pass on my love and best wishes for a happy and successful future for her and her family.

Thank you, K.

Hi Tracy,

Whilst walking through Asda with my mam I passed the book section in hope of finding a new novel to read. I was immediately drawn to the title of your book. My

Acknowledgements

mam told me before purchasing that I may find it difficult to read, due to my age (I'm sixteen) and the content,
but I assured her I'd manage. After racing home from
the shops I was eager to begin reading your story.
Night after night I lay in bed reading page after page,
trying to understand the content of each word. I have
just finished reading your book and I felt I should jump
at the opportunity to express my opinion to you. This
message may never get to you but if it does I can't
thank you enough for taking time to read it. I found
your story very emotional, but I must admit, whilst
reaching the end of the book I was brought to tears by
your sheer determination to raise awareness of this
horrific issue. The events that you have faced throughout your life are those that no child should ever have to
experience, but I can only congratulate you on portray-
ing your own personal trauma in such a way to help
others. You are an inspiration and have taught me so
much.

Too many teenagers these days obsess over who has
the nicest clothes or most modern technology, but
learning there are children worldwide suffering similar to you has been a real eye-opener. It was a topic that
so many people shy away from but you had the courage
to stand up and be counted and I genuinely hope that
there are others who have read this and found comfort
if not a voice in your story.

I have a friend who suffers abuse from her father, not
sexually but physically, but due to my age I never really

fully understood what options were available or believed anyone would listen. My friend has recently slit her legs to try and distract the pain. I try to comfort her as best I can but I know I'm useless. I know and fully understand this is nothing in comparison to what you have been through but I want you to know that I will be giving her your book to read in hope that she too will finally gain the confidence she needs to be able to get away from the issues she is currently facing. Once again I would like to thank you for reading this and I hope I haven't wasted too much of your time. Thank you for all that you have taught me and I am confident that my friend will find comfort in your story.

Love T.

I have just finished reading *Never a Hero to Me* and I have to say what an emotional journey it took me on. I too was abused from an early age, by both my stepbrothers, then I was raped by a school helper and then I was abused by partners; I have also never felt a mother's love, which I too longed for so badly, still do in fact; also my brother was taken as a child and sexually assaulted by a man, and with that and all I have been through I can't look at anyone now without thinking they are a potential paedophile. It ruins my life and my kids' lives but I don't know what to do, I am going to try counselling now I have read the book and I hope that will help me.

Acknowledgements

Thank you so much for the book, it really did help me, LL.

As with *Never a Hero to Me*, I have used a pseudonym to protect myself and my family. I wish this didn't have to be the case, and I sometimes wonder whether I should have fought against all the advice to do this and just accepted the consequences of using my real name, no matter what they may have been, but I had others to think of, and I would never wish any harm to them. However, you can contact me in confidence through my ghostwriter at l.wb@ stampless.co.uk, and I know that messages will be passed on.

I am so very grateful to everyone who has taken the time to contact me. The main reason for telling my story was to speak out against those who abuse children, in all their forms, and to reach those who have also survived horrific childhoods. I hope that I have achieved this and I thank all of you for your encouragement. As I said in my first book, we're the ones who are still standing, we're the heroes.

As always, Linda Watson-Brown has turned my words into the story you have just read. When I first emailed her after reading another survivor memoir she had ghostwritten a few years ago, I never dreamed that she would be able to give such power to what I told her, or that it would reach such a wide audience, but she always said that my story should be heard. I would like to thank her from the bottom of my heart. She has been a tower of strength, she has been patient and, more importantly, she has always listened.

I would like to thank all the educational establishments who gave me self-esteem and confidence as an adult returning to learning. The achievements I made in those places gave me a sense of pride I never expected and which I will cherish forever.